speakout 2ND EDITION

Intermediate Plus
Workbook

with key

T0385843

Caroline Cooke

CONTENTS

CONTENTS

VOCABULARY

LIFESTYLE

1 Complete the article with the words in the box.

nomadic   active   early   alternative   long   sedentary

The wind in my hair

I wasn't one of those children who had always dreamt of being a pilot. I thought I would be more like my parents. They live in an isolated cottage in the countryside, they grow their own vegetables and they don't have a car or a TV. I guess you could say that they have a(n) ¹_____ lifestyle.

So I think they (and I) were quite surprised when I was drawn to the idea of flying. So here I am, leading a somewhat ²_____ existence as a long-haul pilot as I move from place to place, never sleeping in the same bed for more than a couple of days while I'm working. It's strange though; my job is really a ³_____ occupation and I need to do the same as the passengers and get out of my seat occasionally to wander up and down the aircraft and stretch my legs. Once I arrive, I do take care to be more ⁴_____ and get to the hotel gym or go for a swim in the sea if I'm near the coast, but it's sometimes difficult as the ⁵_____ hours we fly mean that I really just want to get to bed. On my days off, I'm definitely a(n) ⁶_____ bird and get out on my bike as the sun rises to feel the wind in my hair – something that never happens on the plane!

2 A Underline the stressed syllables in the words in bold.
1 They led a *nomadic* life.
2 Computer programming is a **sedentary** profession.
3 My working day is very **active**.
4 I like to stick to a **routine**.
5 She's got an **alternative** lifestyle.
6 He was always an **early** bird.

B ▶ 1.1 Listen and check. Then listen again and repeat.

LISTENING

3 A ▶ 1.2 Listen to four people talking about events that brought about important changes in their lives. Match speakers 1–4 with events a)–d).

1	Martha	**a)**	an accident
2	Daniel	**b)**	retirement
3	Jenny	**c)**	a holiday
4	Jack	**d)**	a meeting

B Listen again and answer the questions.
1 What was Martha's previous job?
_____
2 What does Martha do now?
_____
3 Who made Daniel cry?
_____
4 What two things has Daniel done to improve his lifestyle?
_____
5 What two things does Jenny do to deal with her problems?
_____
6 What two things does Jenny do to occupy her time?
_____
7 What was Jack's previous job?
_____
8 What two activities has Jack done recently?
_____

C Read extracts 1–8 from the recording. Match the words/phrases in bold with definitions a)–h).
1 What was a luxury tour in Africa turned into **an eye-opener**.
2 disease caused by **lack** of clean water
3 I just **broke down**.
4 I still **crave** cigarettes.
5 It's been **tough** getting used to the change.
6 **be aware** of the moment
7 I never had a moment **to spare**.
8 I'm able to live life **to the full**.

a) hard
b) free
c) absence
d) notice
e) a surprising discovery
f) completely
g) collapsed emotionally
h) have a strong desire for

GRAMMAR

THE PASSIVE; CAUSATIVE HAVE

4 Rewrite the sentences in the passive.

1 Someone showed her the way to the station.
She was shown the way to the station.

2 Something bit him on his leg.

_____

3 People are doing a lot of work.

_____

4 Scientists have discovered the cure.

_____

5 People make the blankets by hand.

_____

6 They don't allow dogs in the hotel.

_____

5 Complete the blog with the correct form of the verbs in the box and the words in brackets. Use the causative *have*.

| cut   install   make   remove   paint   replace |

👤 sign out   🔍 search

A big project!

The new house was a disaster when my sister and her husband first moved in. There was a lot of renovation needed and they couldn't do it by themselves, so they got some experts in to help them. First, they ¹_____ (the windows) with PVC models because the wooden ones were broken. Afterwards, they ²_____ (the walls) in pastel colours to make the rooms lighter. They threw away the old curtains and ³_____ (new ones) in the little shop on the corner. They are lovely! As for the bathroom, they ⁴_____ (the years of dirt) by a special cleaning company and discovered that the tiles were pale green. Then they ⁵_____ (a new walk-in shower), which is great. Finally, they called a gardener and ⁶_____ (the grass). It looks much better now.

---

6 Find and correct the mistakes in the sentences. Two sentences are correct.

1 A letter has being sent to the head teacher.

2 My sister had her hair cut really short.

3 The photos had been take from an old album.

4 Has been he told about the crime yet?

5 Harvey was vote the best employee of the year.

6 Did you have your nails done in the new shop?

7 The neighbours had a large wall putting up around the garden.

8 The children are been helped by a special tutor this week.

VOCABULARY PLUS

MULTI-WORD VERBS

7 A Underline the correct alternatives to complete the sentences.

1 I need to lose weight, so I'm trying very hard to keep myself *from/to* eating sweet things.

2 The head teacher is retiring next week. She's handing *up/over* to her deputy.

3 Do you think we can put *on/off* the meeting till Tuesday? I'm away till then.

4 We'll have to look *forward to/into* the type of course you could study in the future.

5 I don't want to take *after/on* any more work. I'm overloaded already.

6 Her earrings were handed *over/down* to the eldest daughter in the family.

7 His son takes *after/on* him in looks and temperament.

8 She had put *off/up* with his bad behaviour for years, but finally she left him.

9 This year's been hard. I'm so looking forward *at/to* the holidays.

10 What do you do to keep *on/up* with the news: watch TV or use the internet?

B Complete the sentences with the correct form of multi-word verbs from Exercise 7A.

1 If you live in a student residence, you'll have to _____ a lot of noise.

2 Fashion changes so quickly it's difficult to _____ the latest trends.

3 My niece starts work in the family business next year, so I'll _____ the office administration to her.

4 Do you think your daughter will _____ her grandfather and become a doctor as well?

5 My new puppy loves shoes! I can't _____ him _____ chewing any he finds.

6 I had to _____ my dentist's appointment three times because of urgent meetings at work.

7 Thank you very much for your help and I _____ receiving the order next week.

8 Do you realise you'll have to _____ a lot more responsibility if you become head of department?

VOCABULARY

VERB + PREPOSITION

1 Complete the sentences with the words in the box.

| by   on   out   over   with (x2)   for   around   up |

1 You've been working too hard lately. You should take some time _____ to spend with your family.
2 It's hard having four kids. I spend all day racing _____ with them from one activity to another.
3 He needs to make more time _____ his girlfriend. She feels he doesn't want to be with her.
4 I've let my work pile _____ so much that I can't possibly meet the deadline.
5 The government has got no control _____ the crisis, so the situation is getting worse.
6 My son is struggling _____ maths this year. He just doesn't understand algebra.
7 She's overwhelmed _____ the responsibility of her new job and feels stressed.
8 I don't think I can take _____ any more work this month. I'm too busy.
9 I can't keep up _____ technology. It changes so fast.

2 Replace the words in bold in the sentences with the phrases in the box.

| struggle with   make time for   be overwhelmed by have no control over   pile up   take on take time out   keep up with   race around |

1 I've been so busy recently. I need to **have a break** and go on a yoga retreat.
2 I work full time and I also help at my son's school. I really can't **say yes to** any more responsibilities at the moment.
3 Don't give your email to that website. You'll **find it hard to deal with** the advertising they send you!
4 You'll really have to **go quickly from one place to another** this morning to get all you need for the holiday.
5 He can always **find a moment for** me when I need help.
6 I can't **go at the same speed as** my classmates. They all finish the exercises before me.
7 I haven't had time for housework this week, so I've let the ironing **accumulate**. It'll take me hours to do it!
8 We **can't manage** the situation because no one has given us the authority to act.
9 They **have difficulties** understanding his accent.

3 A Mark the two places in each sentence where the words are linked together.

1 I race_around_doing the shopping.
2 The work is piling up.
3 He took time out to play tennis.
4 Joe's struggling with the course.
5 He had no control over his son.
6 She took on new responsibilities.

B ▶ 1.3 Listen and check. Then listen again and repeat.

GRAMMAR

PRESENT TENSES: SIMPLE VS CONTINUOUS, STATIVE VERBS

4 Underline the correct alternatives to complete the sentences.

1 This project *is taking/takes* me longer to do than usual.
2 You can't borrow my car because I *am needing/ need* it this afternoon.
3 Who *is coming/comes* to your party on Saturday?
4 So, what *do you do/are you doing*? Are you a teacher?
5 The local council *is thinking/thinks* that environmental issues are important.
6 How often *are they visiting/do they visit* you?

5 Complete the conversations with the present simple or present continuous form of the verbs in brackets.

1 A: Why _____ (you/close) the windows?
   B: Because it's going to rain and I _____ (not want) the floor to get wet!
2 A: I _____ (realise) now that you're not happy with the situation and I'm sorry.
   B: Too right! You _____ (forever/ complain) but now it's my turn.
3 A: The government says that prices _____ (fall) but everything _____ (seem) to be more expensive.
   B: That's true. Petrol _____ (cost) five cents more than last year.
4 A: What _____ (you/do) in the mornings now that you have retired?
   B: Well, it _____ (depend) on the weather. Sometimes I _____ (go) for a walk in the park and other days I _____ (prefer) to stay in.
5 A: Sally _____ (stay) the night at our house this Friday.
   B: Oh no! I won't be here. I _____ (go) away for the weekend. I _____ (suppose) I could cancel.
6 A: My son _____ (grow) so quickly. I _____ (constantly/buy) new clothes for him.
   B: I _____ (have) the same problem. Lenny _____ (need) new shoes every couple of months.
7 A: She just _____ (not understand) my problem.
   B: Well, maybe she _____ (not realise) how important it is for you.
8 A: I _____ (need) to get my hair cut.
   B: What _____ (you/wait) for? Make an appointment now!

READING

6 A Read the title of the article. What do you think it means? Choose the best summary. Read and check.

a) How we eat is a way of life.
b) It's better for us to eat slowly.
c) Modern lifestyles give us more eating choices.

B Match headings a)–d) with paragraphs 1–4.

a) What the real supporters do
b) It's more than just eating to live
c) The origins of Slow Food
d) Recommendations for everyone

We are what we eat

It could only be in a country such as Italy, where good food and conversation at the table are such a tradition, that a movement like Slow Food started. What better way to spend your time than eating well in the company of good friends?

1 _____

The Slow Food movement was started in 1989 with the aim of encouraging an interest in food – in both eating itself and in food production. At that time it seemed that fast food was taking over Europe. Restaurant chains were opening in many countries and many people felt that these new trends in eating were changing our lifestyles in a negative way. For example, workers no longer needed long lunch breaks and everyone had to work harder and faster. People became more interested in low prices than quality.

2 _____

Slow Food recommends a lifestyle that thinks of food not only in terms of giving us energy and keeping healthy but also considers where our food comes from. It advises us to support organic agriculture and food producers who try to provide us with quality products. They promote the idea of 'good, clean and fair food' as a philosophy that goes further than eating and is reflected in the way we treat other people and appreciate the world we live in as well.

3 _____

The ways they suggest we can immediately change our lives for the better are relatively easy to act on. Buy locally grown produce, reduce your consumption of fast food and processed food and make eating a social event that you share with other people, not only your direct family. Check where your food has come from and find out if it has been produced by farmers who are treated fairly.

4 _____

It takes a lot of time to be a true Slow Food follower. They grow their own fruit and vegetables and rear their own animals to eat. They eat dishes made from basic ingredients. They also help others to develop community gardens or spend time teaching children about the value of good food and the importance of maintaining eating and cooking traditions. Would you be prepared to change your lifestyle to slow down your relationship with food?

WRITING

AN ARTICLE; LEARN TO USE PERSUASIVE LANGUAGE

7 A Match the tips for using persuasive language 1–3 with the extracts from an article a)–f).

1 Use rhetorical questions to make the reader think.
2 Use personal pronouns to appeal directly to the reader.
3 Convince the reader with facts and figures.

a) You become more aware of …
b) Experts say …
c) What do these apps do?
d) Recent studies have shown that …
e) Who doesn't want to be … ?
f) You'll make new friends.

B Complete the article with phrases a)–f) in Exercise 7A.

● ● ● ‹ ›

Fit but not fanatic 🔍

¹ _____ fitter and healthier? One of the latest trends that has hit the markets is to use technology to help you. Yes, I'm talking about fitness applications.

² _____ Well, they record statistics about the walking, running or cycling you do and help you set realistic targets. You can also compare the calories you consume with the calories you burn to help you lose those extra kilos. That way ³ _____ how you need to change your habits.

They are also easily personalised so you won't overdo the exercise when you start. They can calculate your level of fitness and create a programme for you to follow, which ⁴ _____ will improve your health effectively. Even if you have a sedentary job and little time to do exercise, they will give you a realistic plan you can follow.

What's more, if you are competitive person, there are apps that can be connected to other users, friends, family or even strangers in your area so that you can compare results, set each other challenges and find that extra motivation to improve. Maybe ⁵ _____ this way too!

Using these apps is not just about short-term changes – they really can be life-changing. ⁶ _____ users of these apps have quickly become used to a more active lifestyle. I have had mine for two months now, so you must excuse me – I have to run up the stairs now!

C Look at these philosophies and technologies that can help you change your lifestyle. Choose one, research information if necessary and write an article (200–250 words).

- mindfulness
- feng shui
- digital detox
- time management apps

VOCABULARY
EVERYDAY OBJECTS

1 Write the words in the box in the correct group.

> watch   bank card   coffee pot   doll   laptop
> necklace   bottle opener   ring   skateboard
> ukulele   key   wallet   charger   hard drive

1 two objects you can find in a kitchen cupboard or drawer: _____, _____

2 three objects you can wear: _____, _____, _____

3 three objects you can play or play with: _____, _____, _____

4 three objects related to technology: _____, _____, _____

5 three objects men may have in their pocket: _____, _____, _____

2 Underline the correct alternatives to complete the sentences.

1 A *charger/watch/wallet* is indispensable if you want to know the time.

2 A *wallet/key/laptop* is practical if you want to work on the train.

3 A *hard drive/necklace/bottle opener* is useful if you want a drink.

4 A *bank card/ukulele/wallet* can be made of wood.

5 A skateboard without wheels is *essential/ necessary/pointless*.

6 A *football/necklace/doll* made of glass is impractical.

7 A *letter/diary/packet* is good for writing in.

8 A *sculpture/charger/lead* is necessary to train a dog.

9 A gold ring can be *healthy/valuable/ practical*.

10 A *notebook/cap/clock* can protect your head.

FUNCTION
DESCRIBING EVERYDAY OBJECTS

3 A Complete the sentences and questions. Use one word in each gap.

1 What is it made _____?

2 What is it useful _____?

3 It's _____ bit expensive.

4 It _____ sentimental value.

5 You can _____ it to make cakes.

6 You need it _____ cut the grass.

 A

 B

 C

 D

B ▶ **1.4** Listen and match descriptions 1–4 with photos A–D.

C Listen again and complete the sentences.

1 a) It's not very _____ because it _____ wheels.
   b) It's made of _____.

2 a) It's actually made of some _____.
   b) It has _____ because I got it after a lot of effort.

3 a) It looks _____.
   b) I only use it _____.

4 a) I'm not sure _____ to do with it.
   b) No one _____ it any more.

LEARN TO
RESPOND TO SUGGESTIONS

4 Complete the conversations with the words in the box.

> sure   like   that   must   definitely   kidding
> let's   really   say   think   choice   same

1 A: Well, Mrs Dale, I _____ you should have few days resting at home.
   B: Thank you, doctor. I was thinking the _____ thing.

2 A: Michael, your father and I would _____ you to study law.
   B: Sorry, Mum, but I don't think that would be my first _____.

3 A: We _____ organise the finance before we can plan in detail.
   B: _____. I agree.

4 A: _____ walk up to the next hill.
   B: You're _____! I'm exhausted!

5 A: I'd _____ a book would be a good present.
   B: Does he like reading? I'm not sure about _____.

6 A: Do you _____ think he'll pass his driving test?
   B: I'm not _____. He hasn't had much practice.

VOCABULARY

ADJECTIVES TO DESCRIBE INVENTIONS

1 Complete the advert with the adjectives in the box. Use the definitions in brackets to help you.

> edible   portable   unique   flimsy   biodegradable
> durable   groundbreaking   novel   stunning   clip-on

All you need for a perfect picnic

Eating easily

Are you fed up with ¹_____ (always breaking) plastic knives and forks? Our new ²_____ (will last for years) models can be re-used and their ³_____ (new) design makes it easy to fit them in your basket.

Keeping food cool

Our ⁴_____ (light and easy to carry) fridge is ideal for family picnics. It uses ⁵_____ (innovative) solar technology to keep your food cool on a sunny day so that it's still ⁶_____ (you can eat it) even after several hours.

Keeping clean

Less washing, more fun! Our new range of ⁷_____ (can be attached to clothes) serviettes come in ⁸_____ (very attractive) colours that your children will love. They are ⁹_____ (can be thrown away without harming the environment).

These designs are ¹⁰_____ (only found here) – you won't find them anywhere else. Click <u>here</u> to see and order our products.

READING

2 What do you think are the most important inventions of the past 200 years? Read the article. Does it mention any of your ideas?

3 Read the article again and answer the questions.

1 What did Bell do when communication companies dismissed his invention?

_____

2 Why did de Forest think that television would not be a successful invention?

_____

3 What does the author suggest children liked doing at the turn of the century?

_____

4 Why did some critics decide not to review the iPad when it was launched?

_____

5 What does the author say we need to have in order to recognise genius inventions?

_____

4 Match the words in bold in the article with definitions 1–5.

1 not accepted _____
2 have become more important _____
3 ready or prepared _____
4 possible _____
5 looking at something for a long time _____

CHANGING THE WORLD

Inventors have often been ridiculed when they first suggest a groundbreaking device or idea. From the aeroplane to the first moon landing, critics initially thought the concepts were impossible or would never be a commercial success, but often they were proved wrong. Modern technology has developed from many ideas that were originally regarded as absurd.

The nineteenth and twentieth centuries

Let's start with the telephone. Invented by Alexander Graham Bell in the 1870s, his device was **rejected** by communications companies at the time as being no more than a toy. The head of the British Post Office even asked why we would need such a gadget when telegrams and the messenger service, where couriers directly transported important written messages, worked so well. Bell had to found his own company to produce his invention.

And then there's television. In the early 1900s an American inventor, Lee De Forest, who is known as 'the grandfather of television' because of his inventions in sound recording technology, actually said, 'While theoretically and technically television may be **feasible**, commercially and financially it is an impossibility, a development of which we need waste little time dreaming.' Even as late as 1946 one movie producer said, 'People will get tired of **staring** at a plywood box every night.' Tell that to the parents of children at the turn of this century!

The twenty-first century

Can you imagine a modern home without a PC? In the early days of computers, few could predict how computers would be used at home. Nowadays we can't live without them unless you have a smartphone that does everything for you – another unimaginable idea a few years ago! And amongst the young, watching

a computer screen has **overtaken** the TV as a free time activity.

Do you remember when the iPad was launched in 2010? The idea was to create a device that was more portable than a computer but easier to use for sending emails and browsing the internet than a smartphone. At the time, Bill Gates thought it was 'nice', but nothing special. Some critics thought it wasn't even worth reviewing and predicted that it would be a failure, but it turned out to be a huge success.

Scared of change?

Why do people often reject innovation? It may be because they are afraid of change – they prefer what they know or it may be that they are not **willing** to take risks, particularly financial risks. Or maybe it's because they like to find fault and lack imagination. While you are reading this, amazing ideas are being thought up which will, no doubt, change our world.

GRAMMAR
QUESTION FORMS; INDIRECT QUESTIONS

5 Find and correct the mistakes in the sentences. Two sentences are correct.

1 Could you tell me where is the bathroom?
2 Do you know if he's coming tomorrow?
3 Who did design that building?
4 How many people do live in this house?
5 Do you remember where does he live?
6 Can you tell me when she went home?
7 Why he bought that strange machine?
8 Do you know why did he leave his job?

6 Write questions for the underlined information in the answers.

1 *Where was he living in 1985?*
   In 1985 he was living <u>in Manchester</u>.
2 _____
   She should tell him <u>the answer</u>.
3 _____
   She visited <u>her cousins</u> last Sunday.
4 _____
   <u>Only two</u> families live in the apartment block.
5 _____
   They take the dog out <u>every morning</u>.
6 _____
   His grandmother left him <u>10,000 pounds</u>.

7 Rewrite the questions as indirect questions.

1 When did she leave the party?
   Can you tell me *when she left the party* ?
2 How often do you shop in this mall?
   Can I ask _____ ?
3 Why does he get home so late every day?
   Can you tell me _____ ?
4 Are they going to finish on time?
   Could you tell me _____ ?
5 Who have you invited for dinner?
   Can I ask _____ ?
6 Will you be available tomorrow?
   Can you tell me _____ ?

8 A ▶ 2.1 Listen and decide which of the statements are questions. Put a question mark after the statement questions.

1 Her son made that model. He's very talented.
2 She's got three daughters.
3 They've already been to Paris.
4 He's fifty. He doesn't look that old.
5 You thought it was good.

B Listen again and repeat. Copy the intonation.

WRITING
A PRODUCT DESCRIPTION; LEARN TO WRITE PERSUASIVE COPY

9 A Underline the correct alternatives to complete the advert.

> **Tantam Total Cream** is the world's ¹*most/more* effective wrinkle remover.
>
> Specially ²*creating/created* for mature skin, you will see results in less than a month.
>
> It contains tea tree oil, which is ³*truly/actually* refreshing and ⁴*enhances/provides* your complexion.
>
> So why ⁵*not/don't* try a free sample today from your local store? Be ⁶*sure/clear* to use this coupon!
>
> TANTAM TOTAL CREAM WRINKLE REMOVER
>
> **Special offer! Free!**   Tantam Total Cream
> Redeemable in all participating stores
> Offer valid till end March

B The advert in Exercise 9A uses the following structure. Look back at the advert and match sections 1–4 with questions a)–d).

1 introduction   a) What should you do right now?
2 main details   b) Who is the product for?
3 further information c) What is the product for?
4 closing incentive d) What is the product made of?

10 Read the product description below. Match tips a)–e) for writing persuasive copy with the words/phrases in bold in the product description.

a) Explain the benefits of the product.
b) Use adjectives that appeal to the reader's emotions.
c) Use rhetorical questions to attract the reader's attention.
d) Give details of what the product is like.
e) Use superlative language.

> ¹**Are you looking for** the ultimate in comfortable sports shoes?
>
> You need go no further than DV Sportswear. Our special offer, for this week only, is DVX men's and women's running shoes. Using breathable fabric to keep your feet drier and cushioned soles for comfort, they come in both ²**slim fit and wide fit models**.
>
> For either regular walking or jogging, you'll need the support these shoes can offer. These ³**stylish** trainers, with their bold colourful design, will make you stand out from the crowd.
>
> This high-quality, durable product is the ⁴**best** value for money and ⁵**will protect** your feet for miles and miles.

11 Write a product description for something you own that you want to sell on a website (100–150 words). Use the ideas in Exercise 10B and the tips in Exercise 11.

VOCABULARY

BUILDINGS

1 A Put the letters in brackets in the correct order to complete the sentences with words for buildings.

1 When I was a child, we used to play in the _____ (narb) on my grandfather's farm.

2 The _____ (globwuan) has only one floor, so it's easy to move from one room to another.

3 One of the finest buildings in the city is the _____ (aldchetra), which is still used for religious services.

4 Residents are opposing the plans for a textile _____ (ryafotc) because they think it will contaminate the river.

5 Although it's cold, my plants are doing well in the _____ (srgeheueno).

6 The explorers made a _____ (tresleh) from tree branches, where they spent the night.

7 The explosion occurred in a _____ (urohwaese) where they kept fireworks and other explosives.

8 The energy company chose a _____ (dimliwnl) as their symbol because they specialise in wind turbines.

B Complete the sentences with words from Exercise 1A.

1 The old _____ on the hill was used in the past to grind wheat to make flour.

2 We've got a small _____ in the garden where we grow tomatoes.

3 There's a large _____ next to the farmhouse where they keep the tractors.

4 The company has a _____ where they store the goods before distribution.

5 My grandfather can't manage stairs any more, so he's going to live in a _____.

6 I can't believe you got married in a _____! You must have good connections in the church.

7 He's homeless, but he's made a cardboard _____ in the park where he sleeps.

8 They're planning to build a car _____ near the town, which will provide jobs for the locals.

2 A ▶ 2.2 Listen to six sentences and number words a)–f) in the order you hear them.

a) castle _____ **d)** mosque _____
b) school _____ **e)** design _____
c) island _____ **f)** architect _____

B ▶ 2.3 Listen and repeat the words from Exercise 2A. Underline the silent letters.

LISTENING

3 Look at the photos. What kind of building do they show?

4 A ▶ 2.4 Listen to a radio interview about an unusual competition. What is the competition called?

B How do people in Britain use their sheds? Tick the ways you heard.

1 as a storage space for garden tools
2 as a place to sleep
3 as a place to escape to
4 as an art studio
5 as a children's play area
6 as a dining room
7 as a bathroom
8 as a shop

C Listen again and circle the correct answer, a), b) or c).

1 What do some men avoid doing after meals?
   a) storing tools   **b)** washing-up
   c) clearing the table

2 What do women often do to their sheds that men maybe don't do?
   a) decorate them   **b)** personalise them
   c) rebuild them

3 What have some people set up in their shed?
   a) a school   **b)** a business   **c)** a club

4 What do the sheds in the competition have in common?
   a) They are unique.   **b)** They have wooden walls.
   c) They are ecological.

5 What recycled materials have some people used to make their sheds?
   a) plastic   **b)** paper   **c)** cartons

6 Who decides the winner of the Shed of the Year competition?
   a) the owners   **b)** the judges   **c)** the public

7 What is more popular in a shed than a wheelbarrow?
   a) wi-fi   **b)** a fridge   **c)** a TV

8 According to psychologists, what elements improve productivity in the workplace?
   a) light and ventilation
   b) light and comfortable furniture
   c) light and warmth

GRAMMAR
PRESENT PERFECT SIMPLE AND CONTINUOUS

5 Underline the correct alternatives to complete the sentences.

1 How often have you *visited/been visiting* London?
2 The snow has *fallen/been falling* for hours, so we can't go out.
3 Who has *taken/been taking* the last biscuit?
4 I've *painted/been painting* a lot of pictures in my life.
5 You must be tired; you should stop now. You've *worked/been working* since 6 o'clock this morning.
6 How long have you *known/been knowing* Lisa?
7 She has *spent/been spending* six years in Spain.
8 My hands are really dirty because I've *repaired/been repairing* the car all afternoon.

6 Complete the email with the verb forms in the box.

> have certainly been   have been staying
> have been having   have been working   have given
> have had   have finally found   have helped

| To | Gwen | From | Rebecca |

Hi Gwen,

How are you? Well, I ¹_____ time to write to you! Things ²_____ busy since I arrived here in Berlin. It's an amazing place. I ³_____ in a hotel for the past two weeks but I hope to get a flat soon. Work is going well. They ⁴_____ me my own office and I ⁵_____ with another intern. My co-workers are really friendly and we ⁶_____ a couple of evenings out together. I ⁷_____ problems with the language though. German is more difficult than I expected. Still, my colleagues ⁸_____ me find a teacher, so I should pick it up soon.

More later!
Love, Rebecca

7 Complete the conversations with the past simple, present perfect simple or present perfect continuous form of the verbs in brackets.

1 **A:** What's that smell?
   B: I _____ (paint) the living room.
      I _____ (nearly/finish).
   A: Where _____ (buy) the paint?
      I _____ (never/smell) anything like it!
   B: I _____ (get) it from the new hardware store that _____ (just/open) in the mall.
2 **A:** _____ (you/see) my car keys?
      I _____ (look) for them for ages.
   B: No. _____ (you/try) looking in the bedroom? I _____ (find) them under the bed when you lost them last week.
   A: I certainly _____ (not leave) them there.
   B: Are you sure you _____ (not put) them in your bag last night?
   A: Oh yes! Here they are!

VOCABULARY *PLUS*
WORD-BUILDING: PREFIXES AND SUFFIXES

8 A Add a suffix to the words in the box to make adjectives. Write the adjectives in the correct place in the table.

> skill   poison   help   change   do   green   joy
> origin   courage   reason   region   mountain
> child   music   fifty

-al	-ful	-ous	-ish	-able

B Complete the sentences with adjectives from Exercise 8A.

1 The experts examined the painting and found that it wasn't a(n) _____, only a good copy.
2 It's a(n) _____ moment for the family when a child is born.
3 Why do you still play such _____ games? You're an adult now!
4 The village is very _____ and remote, so not many people live there.
5 This crossword isn't _____ because the clues are too difficult.
6 It was very _____ of you to risk your life to save the boy.

9 A Match prefixes 1–5 with meanings a)–e).

1 co-   a) again, repeated
2 mid-   b) with
3 mis-   c) wrongly, incorrectly
4 re-   d) negative
5 dis-   e) in the middle of

B Add prefixes from Exercise 9A to the words in brackets to complete the text.

| sign in | search |

It's sometimes difficult having a sister like mine. She's a famous actress, currently ¹_____ (starring) in a film with Emma Thompson and she loves the celebrity lifestyle. We're very different. I'm very tidy and she's totally ²_____ (organised), so it was difficult to ³_____ (exist) when we shared a flat for a while. Another problem is that we look alike and sometimes people ⁴_____ (take) me for her, which can be annoying. Plus, she's always busy, so I hardly ever see her. Last week she finally had a moment to come over but when she arrived, it was already ⁵_____ (afternoon), about 4.30. I thought she was coming straight after lunch but maybe I had ⁶_____ (understood) because she's always ⁷_____ (scheduling) appointments. She apologised and said she was late because they had had to ⁸_____ (do) a scene ten times that morning. Still, I was happy to see her! After all, she *is* my sister!

VOCABULARY

PROJECTS

1 Circle the correct answer, a), b) or c), to complete the sentences.

1 We'll need to find a _____ to get funds to set up the factory.
a) budget   **b)** promotion
c) sponsor

2 Have you found a _____ for the event yet?
a) venue   **b)** equipment
c) management

3 The most important factor in a good hotel is the _____ that provide the service.
a) tool   **b)** business
c) personnel

4 We have a good _____ for the school this year, thanks to a donation.
a) budget   **b)** financing
c) publicity

5 My brother is working on _____ funds for the local homeless shelter.
a) needing   **b)** raising
c) calling

6 If you get good marks, the university will give you a _____ for your living expenses.
a) grant   **b)** cut
c) fund

7 An article in the paper about the company is always good _____.
a) publicity   **b)** advertisement
c) event

8 He organises the _____ of the company, such as transport and distribution.
a) funding   **b)** equipment
c) logistics

9 We're on a very tight _____. Everything has to be done by Monday.
a) time   **b)** schedule
c) promotion

10 I can't _____ a new car, so I'll have to borrow some money.
a) promote   **b)** finance
c) sponsor

FUNCTION

JUDGING AND EVALUATING IDEAS

2 A ▶ 2.5 Listen and match conversations 1–6 with pictures A–F.
1 _____   **2** _____   **3** _____   **4** _____   **5** _____   **6** _____

B Listen again and complete the phrases used in each conversation.
1 I like the _____.
2 How does _____?
3 That's a _____.
4 That might _____.
5 I have my _____ about that.
6 That seems like a _____.

C Listen again and underline the correct alternatives to complete the sentences.

1 The businessman is *pleased/unhappy* with the new model being developed.
2 The man *completely agrees with/is doubtful about* the woman's suggestion.
3 The second woman *agrees/disagrees* with the boys' proposal.
4 The woman thinks the man's suggestion is *a possible/an impossible* solution.
5 The man *likes/dislikes* the government's proposal.
6 The businessmen *agree/disagree* about the best place to store the fruit.

LEARN TO

GIVE PRAISE

3 Put the letters in brackets in the correct order to complete the conversations.

1 A: Have you heard that Joe has got a scholarship to university?
B: That's _____ (sitcatfna)!

2 A: The funding for our project has been approved.
B: _____ (leecxltne)! So we can start tomorrow.

3 A: I've just been promoted.
B: _____ (olsumrvale)! You deserve it.

4 A: We got top marks for the new design.
B: _____ (moaswee)! You have worked hard.

5 A: I won first prize in the race.
B: That's _____ (izganam)! You'll be in the Olympics next.

6 A: My maths teacher said I was the best in the class.
B: _____ (rfwodelnu)! I'm so proud of you.

7 A: I've managed to fix your bike.
B: _____ (abnliilrt)! Let's go for a ride.

VOCABULARY LIFESTYLE

1 Complete the sentences. Use one adjective in each gap.

1 People who have _____ jobs, such as office workers, need to make sure they get up and move every so often.

2 The ambulance staff work _____ hours, often doing fourteen-hour shifts.

3 I don't mind you phoning me at 8a.m. You know I'm a(n) _____ bird – I'll be up at seven.

4 So, your hobbies include running, skiing and water polo. You do have a(n) _____ lifestyle!

5 The desert people lead a(n) _____ life, moving in search of water every few days.

6 The documentary discusses ways of _____ living, such as going to live in a Buddhist community.

GRAMMAR THE PASSIVE; CAUSATIVE HAVE

2 Complete the second sentence so that it means the same as the first. Use up to four words.

1 They have told me to come to this hospital.
I _have been told_ to come to this hospital.

2 A professional plumber repaired the sink for me.
I _____ by a professional plumber.

3 Someone sent me an anonymous message.
I _____ an anonymous message.

4 No one said anything about payment for the service.
Nothing _____ about payment for the service.

5 People throw rubbish into the wrong container.
Rubbish _____ into the wrong container.

6 I asked a mechanic to look at the brakes.
I _____ at by a mechanic.

7 Someone made a dress for Jo when she was in Spain.
Jo _____ when she was in Spain.

8 The police may charge him with obstruction.
He _____ with obstruction.

VOCABULARY PLUS MULTI-WORD VERBS

3 Complete the sentences with the correct form of the verbs in the box. You need to use some verbs more than once.

keep	put	take	hand	look

1 He has just _____ over the position of marketing director – his predecessor retired.

2 I expect to _____ over the business to my partner in a few years.

3 You can't keep _____ off going to the dentist. No more excuses!

4 The queen _____ the throne down to her second son before she died.

5 The police are _____ into the case of the stolen jewels.

6 I find it difficult to _____ up with the changes in technology.

VOCABULARY VERB + PREPOSITION

4 Circle the correct answer, a), b) or c) to complete the sentences.

1 She's _____ by the number of emails she gets – over 200 a day!
a) struggled   b) overwhelmed   c) taken

2 You need to make time _____ yourself and do things you enjoy.
a) to   b) for   c) at

3 I've let the electricity bills _____ up and now I can't pay them all.
a) grow   b) work   c) pile

4 He's got no control _____ his dog – it bit the delivery boy.
a) over   b) on   c) with

5 She _____ on a new cleaning job to get some extra money.
a) took   b) carried   c) kept

6 This summer I want to take some time _____ to travel before I start university.
a) over   b) out   c) for

7 You don't need to race _____ so much trying to do everything – I can help you.
a) around   b) along   c) out

8 My grandmother is _____ with her new TV. She can't make it work.
a) running   b) annoying   c) struggling

GRAMMAR PRESENT TENSES

5 Complete the report with the present simple or present continuous form of the verbs in brackets.

... ...

new save edit   share

This report [1]_____ (give) our findings for the company in the first six months of business. At the moment we [2]_____ (make) good progress because the market [3]_____ (grow) and we [4]_____ (have) good prospects for next year. Our customers [5]_____ (know) that we provide quality services. However, there has been a problem with the printers in the second factory that [6]_____ (constantly/break down). It [7]_____ (seem) that the workers [8]_____ (not realise) that the machines [9]_____ (require) regular maintenance. We have found that they [10]_____ (often/leave) them on all night, but we [11]_____ (do) our best to solve these issues. Next week we [12]_____ (hold) training sessions for all staff.

FUNCTION DESCRIBING EVERYDAY OBJECTS

6 Complete the descriptions of objects with the words/
phrases in the box. There are three extra words/
phrases. Then circle the object which is being
described, a), b) or c).

> practical   sentimental   a bit heavy   need it to
> a bit old-fashioned   not too difficult   made of
> no good for   use it when   use it for

A
My favourite one was given to me by my
grandmother, but I do have a more modern
version as well. I ¹_____ people come for
lunch and I want something pretty to put on the
table afterwards. It's ceramic, so it's ²_____,
but if I don't fill it too much, it's ³_____
to carry. I also have some matching cups that are
irreplaceable, so I look after them carefully.
a) a coffee pot   **b)** a sculpture **c)** a penknife

B
Although it may seem strange, mine has real
⁴_____ value for me because my sister
gave it to me for my twenty-first birthday.
Nowadays it's ⁵_____ but I don't
⁶_____ more than calling friends as I use
my laptop for everything else. Oh, and I
⁷_____ tell the time as well!
a) a phone   **b)** a watch   **c)** a charger

LEARN TO RESPOND TO SUGGESTIONS

7 Complete the conversations with sentences a)–e).
A: Joan, we really need a new sofa for the living room.
B: ¹____
A: I've got a catalogue here from the store. Do you
want to have a look at it with me?
B: ²____
A: Oh, I'm not sure about that. It isn't very practical
and red isn't my colour.
B: ³____
A: Why would you choose that? It looks really
uncomfortable. I'd say we should go for this one
made of leather.
B: ⁴____
A: Ah! Here's one that's a reasonable price and a nice
colour too.
B: ⁵____
A: Sure. Let's go this weekend.

a) Maybe you're right. How about this one with
wooden arms?
b) Hmm … let me see. It looks OK. Shall we go to the
store and check it out?
c) OK, great. Ooh! Look at this red velvet one! Isn't it
gorgeous?
d) Are you joking? It's so expensive!
e) I was thinking the same thing.

VOCABULARY ADJECTIVES TO DESCRIBE INVENTIONS

8 Complete the adjectives in the sentences.
1 That phone cover was very fl_____. It broke
after a few days.
2 His gr_____ work into cancer research has
led to the new drug being produced.
3 I've just bought cl_____ lights for my bike
that I can attach to the wheels.
4 The detergent is bi_____ and
environmentally friendly.
5 Don't eat those berries. I don't think they are
ed_____, so they might make you feel ill.
6 The tablet can be used as a po_____
television so you can watch it wherever you are.

GRAMMAR QUESTION FORMS; INDIRECT QUESTIONS

9 Complete the indirect questions.
1 A: Can you tell me _____?
B: The bathroom is through that door on the left.
2 A: Would you tell me _____?
B: We took the photo for the school magazine.
3 A: Do you remember _____?
B: No, I've no idea. Maybe I bought it last year.
4 A: Can I ask _____?
B: I'm forty-five years old.
5 A: Do you know _____?
B: Yes, the ticket costs five pounds.
6 A: Can you tell me _____?
B: He calls me once a week.

VOCABULARY BUILDINGS

10 Read the descriptions and write the types of
building.
1 I can't imagine living there because it's so dark and
cold. Being underground and having no windows
must be horrible. _____
2 The walls are round, so it's difficult to find furniture
that will fit, but it's in a beautiful location on the
top of a hill. I suppose it was built there to catch the
wind when it was working. _____
3 It's outside the city centre, so it's cheaper than
using a central location to store your products.
_____
4 I've never seen such a magnificent structure. It's
taller than any other building in the city and visitors
can go there to admire the architecture or to pray.
_____
5 We keep the food for the animals here and there's
space for the tractor too. _____
6 It's quite old now and some of the glass is broken,
but I used to grow plants in it in the winter.
_____

GRAMMAR PRESENT PERFECT SIMPLE AND CONTINUOUS

11 Complete the letter with the present perfect simple or present perfect continuous form of the verbs in brackets.

Dear Alice,

Great news! We ¹_____ (move) into our new house. To be more precise, we ²_____ (live) here for a week now and I love it! There's a lot to do with the property but we ³_____ (already/begin) the renovations. Over the last week I ⁴_____ (paint) the bedrooms and I ⁵_____ (nearly/finish) both of them. The bathroom is a bit old-fashioned but we ⁶_____ (choose) to only change the shower for the moment and leave the rest. The kitchen was a disaster and Jack ⁷_____ (take) out the old cupboards little by little. He ⁸_____ (not do) them all yet, so we can't eat there. We ⁹_____ (cook) in the living room, using a little gas stove. Meanwhile, the children ¹⁰_____ (start) at their new school and come home every day with stories about who they ¹¹_____ (meet) and what they ¹²_____ (do) all day.

You must come and see us. (When we have a kitchen!)

Lots of love,

Theresa

VOCABULARY PLUS WORD-BUILDING: PREFIXES AND SUFFIXES

12 Add a prefix or suffix to the words in brackets to complete the sentences.

1 The government is feeling _____ (hope) that the economy will improve next year.
2 If your computer freezes, you can _____ (set) it using this button.
3 Some important _____ (universe) human rights are freedom, equality and education.
4 The player broke his ankle _____ (match), so they had to stop the game and take him to hospital.
5 The politician tried to _____ (inform) the press by telling lies about his part in the scandal.
6 If you make a mistake, you'll have to _____ (do) the whole project.
7 Did you _____ (hear) what I asked you to do? Why have you done it wrong?
8 Be careful because there are several species of _____ (poison) snakes in the area.
9 I think my students are _____ (interested) in the subject because they never pay attention.
10 My job is made easier because my _____ (workers) are so great to work with.

VOCABULARY PROJECTS

13 Complete the sentences with the words in the box.

schedule   fundraising   promotion   budget
equipment   financing   publicity   grants
venue   sponsors

1 We can use part of our annual _____ to pay for the new offices.
2 You shouldn't go rock-climbing without the correct safety _____.
3 The supermarket has a new _____: two for the price of one on most products.
4 They've chosen a really good _____ for the concert that is easy to get to on public transport.
5 My new boss has changed the _____ for the project, so we have even less time to complete it.
6 The government is offering _____ for disadvantaged students who want to study abroad.
7 Do you think you'll get _____ from the bank for your project?
8 Running a marathon is a good way of _____ for charity.
9 We forgot to put their name on the T-shirts, so our _____ are not happy.
10 You should include TV and radio adverts as part of your _____ campaign.

FUNCTION JUDGING AND EVALUATING IDEAS

14 Cross out four extra words in each conversation.

1 A: So, what do you think about our project?
   B: I'm sure it has a potential. You've got some great ideas, but maybe you should to redo the schedule. I think you're a bit too much optimistic about the time it's going to take.
   A: How about three weeks instead of two? How does that may sound?
   B: Probably better, just to be safe.
2 A: So where are we going to get financing for this?
   B: I thought we could try on the local council. They offer grants for young entrepreneurs.
   A: That might be work. When do we need to apply?
   B: The deadline is next week.
   A: There's no any way we can get it organised by then!
   B: So, it's being out of the question. We'll have to think of somewhere else.
3 A: I reckon the best venue for the graffiti exhibition is an art gallery.
   B: Well, that's might a possibility, but won't it be expensive?
   A: You're probably with right. What about the local youth centre?
   B: That's a one non-starter. You know the council don't like graffiti.
   A: OK. Let's to look on the internet for other possibilities.

CHECK

Circle the correct answer, a), b) or c), to complete the sentences.

1 You should avoid a lifestyle that is too _____ if you want to keep your weight down.
   a) sedentary   **b)** active   **c)** nomadic

2 We need to _____ into Chinese. Do you know any good translators?
   a) have translated a report
   b) have a report translated
   c) have translate a report

3 When _____?
   a) was reported the robbery
   b) had the robbery reported
   c) was the robbery reported

4 The new TV _____ delivered this afternoon.
   a) is   **b)** is being   **c)** is been

5 SuperChain is going to take _____ the smaller supermarket in the town.
   a) after   **b)** over   **c)** up

6 There's no train, so she has to put _____ with daily traffic jams to get to work.
   a) off   **b)** up   **c)** on

7 During the crisis, control was _____ over to the army.
   a) handed   **b)** taken   **c)** looked

8 She's completely _____ by running such a large company.
   a) raced   **b)** struggled   **c)** overwhelmed

9 Don't let your homework pile _____ until the last minute. Do some now!
   a) by   **b)** over   **c)** up

10 Even if you have a lot of work, you should _____ time for your family.
   a) take   **b)** make   **c)** tell

11 The delegates _____ the Prime Minister tomorrow to discuss the problem.
   a) are seeing   **b)** see   **c)** have seen

12 I like John but he _____ to like me very much.
   a) isn't seeming   **b)** not seems   **c)** doesn't seem

13 A calculator is _____ for the maths exam.
   a) definite   **b)** pointless   **c)** indispensable

14 You can use this paper for _____ notes.
   a) making   **b)** make   **c)** to make

15 The hurricane destroyed the _____ wooden houses.
   a) flexible   **b)** flimsy   **c)** groundbreaking

16 Is this plastic _____ enough to use to make furniture?
   a) portable   **b)** durable   **c)** unique

17 Do you know why _____ two days off work?
   a) does he want   **b)** do he want   **c)** he wants

18 Can you tell me where _____ that evening?
   a) did she go   **b)** she went   **c)** did she went

19 Who _____ my phone number?
   a) did give you   **b)** did you gave   **c)** gave you

20 The new film stars the world's _____ actor, Sam Brook.
   a) funniest   **b)** funnier   **c)** funny

21 The refugees have made _____ out of plastic boards.
   a) shelters   **b)** barns   **c)** factories

22 The children _____ in the garden and their clothes are filthy!
   a) have played   **b)** have been playing
   c) have being played

23 The artist _____ two paintings so far this week and hopes to sell more before the weekend.
   a) sold   **b)** has sold
   c) has been selling

24 I _____ where I put my address book. Can you help me find it?
   a) forgot   **b)** have forgotten
   c) have been forgetting

25 He _____ the timetable and was late for the train.
   a) misread   **b)** disread   **c)** reread

26 The final scene was very _____ and we all cried.
   a) emotioned   **b)** emotionable   **c)** emotional

27 I think we need to _____ the schedule. We'll never keep to the current dates.
   a) cowork   **b)** rework   **c)** miswork

28 They received a substantial _____ from the local authorities to start the business.
   a) fundraising   **b)** grant   **c)** venue

29 It's difficult to find a _____ for research projects these days.
   a) promotion   **b)** budget   **c)** sponsor

30 I'm not _____ about that.
   a) convinced   **b)** doubts   **c)** possible

RESULT   /30

3)) CHALLENGES

LISTENING

1 A ▶ **3.1 Listen to the introduction to a radio programme about the achievements of sportspeople overcoming learning difficulties. Answer the questions.**

1 Which learning difficulty does Clare Ellis specialise in?

_____

2 How did Clare's pupils feel about their abilities?

_____

3 What two qualities does Clare think are more important than doing well in the classroom?

_____

B ▶ **3.2 What do you know about these sportsmen? Are the statements true (T) or false (F)? Listen to the rest of the programme to check your answers.**

Michael Phelps:

1 is a gymnast. ___

2 won an Olympic medal when he was fifteen . ___

3 hated swimming as a child. ___

Muhammad Ali:

4 was a boxer. ___

5 wrote poetry. ___

6 wasn't self-confident. ___

C Listen again and circle the correct answer, a), b) or c).

1 ADHD affects children's ability to
   a) read.   **b)** concentrate.   **c)** fight.

2 Apart from being a good sportsman, Muhammad Ali was good at
   a) maths.   **b)** business.   **c)** speaking.

3 When he was a child, Michael Phelps was told that he
   a) wasn't hyperactive.
   b) would never be successful.
   c) was terrible.

4 Swimming helped him use up energy and
   a) keep him safe.
   b) increase his strength.
   c) think more calmly.

5 These people can teach us that it's important to try new things and
   a) learn more.
   b) keep trying.
   c) make mistakes.

6 Parents need to help children
   a) follow a traditional path.
   b) experience new activities.
   c) develop their talents.

GRAMMAR

NARRATIVE TENSES

2 Underline the correct alternatives to complete the text.

sign out   search

A photo that caused trouble

Years ago, when I ¹*was/had been* a student, I used to hitchhike around the country because I ²*wasn't having//didn't have* much money to pay for transport. One day I ³*set off/was setting off* to go to

a concert and ⁴*walked/was walking* out to the edge of town to try and get a lift. My mother ⁵*didn't approve/hadn't approved* of hitchhiking, so I ⁶*was telling/had told* her that I ⁷*took/was taking* the train. I ⁸*was waiting/waited* for a car to come when a girl ⁹*approached/was approaching* me and asked if she could take my photo. I was rather surprised, but she ¹⁰*had explained/explained* that she ¹¹*took/was taking* photos of typical students for an article about student life. I agreed and after she ¹²*was taking/had taken* the photo, I ¹³*thought/was thinking* no more about it. I went on to the concert and ¹⁴*got/had got* a lift home again without any problems. It was only two weeks later that my mother ¹⁵*had come/came* to me with the local paper and there was my picture! I ¹⁶*stood/was standing* by the side of the road with my thumb out. She was furious!

3 Underline the correct alternatives to complete the sentences.

1 After sending the email, she *had realised/realised* she *was copying in/had copied in* the wrong person.

2 Before he *joined/was joining* the First Division, he *wins/had won* several trophies in the Junior League.

3 We *were living/had lived* in the city centre when the war *started/starts*.

4 My father *was warning/had warned* me about living in that area, but I *move/moved* there anyway.

5 Although he *had studied/was studied* hard for his exam, he *was failing/failed*.

6 She *was looking/looked* for her ring when she *found/had found* the old letters.

7 I *grew up/was grown up* in a small village where everyone *was knowing/knew* each other.

8 I *was waking up/woke up* in the middle of the night because my phone *was ringing/was rung* loudly in the other room.

9 He *was hurting/hurt* his leg while he *was skiing/skied* last month.

10 They *were arranging/had arranged* to meet in the café but when he *was getting/got* there, it was closed.

VOCABULARY

ADVERBS

4 Complete the sentences with the words in the box.

realistically desperately amazingly cheerfully literally undoubtedly bravely typically

1 She _____ wanted to succeed. In fact, nothing was more important to her.

2 He _____ faced the attacker who was threatening his son.

3 The members of the Masai tribe are _____ tall and thin.

4 Winning the gold medal in the London Olympics was _____ the highlight of her career.

5 She sang _____ as she packed her suitcase to go on holiday.

6 The boy is _____ good at the piano, considering he's only three years old.

7 There were _____ thousands of people on the streets waiting for the king to go by.

8 _____, you can't expect to win the lottery.

WRITING

A BIOGRAPHY; LEARN TO USE LINKERS

5 Complete the sentences with the words in the box.

however although whereas consequently furthermore despite

1 He'd never played in public before. _____, he didn't feel nervous.

2 _____ he had had a difficult childhood, he was a great father.

3 Her coach was very supportive _____ her teammates didn't believe in her.

4 Yoga is recommended to footballers as a good way to relax. _____, it has also been shown to prevent injuries.

5 He was in the lead but then he fell in the last few metres. _____, he didn't win the gold medal.

6 _____ living in a dangerous area, he never felt threatened.

6 A Read the text below and put the paragraphs in the correct order according to these headings.

1 Introduction _____
2 Background/Early life _____
3 Major achievements _____
4 Final comments _____

Tom Daley

A Tom first showed talent at the age of only seven, when he joined his first diving club in his home town, Plymouth. [1]_____ he started secondary school, he had already won several international championships. [2]_____ much of his time was spent training, he managed to get good grades at school. Being famous was not easy and he was bullied at school. [3]_____, he bravely tried to help other children who were having a hard time at school. [4]_____, he also supports The Brain Tumour Charity due to his father's death from this disease when Tom was just seventeen.

B He is admired because he is a skilful diver and is extremely confident, [5]_____ he is also humble and has never let fame go to his head. He's undoubtedly one to watch in this spectacular sport.

C British sportsman Tom Daley is a likeable figure, well-known for his achievements [6]_____ his rise from brilliant junior diver to diving superstar. Still young, he has shown great expertise at the highest level of the sport.

D [7]_____ his disappointment when he missed out on an individual medal in the 2016 Olympics, he didn't give up and went on to win gold in the 2017 World Championships. He has obtained numerous other gold medals in national and international events. He is also a TV celebrity and has appeared on shows such as *Splash!*, where he taught celebrities to dive.

B Complete the text in Exercise 6A with the words in the box.

since despite although by the time because of this in addition to this but

7 Write a short biography (200–250 words) of tennis player Novak Djokovic. Use some of the information below and any other information you can find on the internet or in books.

- born 1987 (Belgrade, Serbia); started playing age 4; tennis courts opposite his parents' restaurant
- war in Belgrade 1999; practised in empty swimming pool because of bombing
- 2008 won Australian Open (6 wins in total); 2011 became no.1 in the world; 2 US Open; 3 Wimbledon titles; many other wins
- great sense of humour; many television appearances
- started a foundation to help disadvantaged children; member of Champions for Peace club – peace through sport
- married 2014; first child 2014; second child 2017
- intolerant to wheat, dairy and tomatoes; only drinks warm water, not cold; ate grass after winning Wimbledon

GRAMMAR

MODALS OF OBLIGATION: PRESENT/ PAST

1 Underline the correct alternatives to complete the sentences.

1 Visitors *must/shouldn't* register with security before entering the main building.

2 You *don't have to/shouldn't* be watching TV now. You've got a lot of homework to do.

3 Why are you at home? You *don't have to/ should* be at work now!

4 I'm happy we *mustn't/don't have to* get up early on Saturday. I need to rest.

5 You *should/don't have to* leave yet. There's lots of time before the train goes.

6 You *mustn't/should* move while I'm taking the photo or the picture will be out of focus.

7 The school rule is that children *mustn't/ don't have to* leave the school without an adult if they are under fourteen.

8 You *should/mustn't* book the tickets today. It may be too late tomorrow.

9 You *don't have to/must* turn off all electronic devices when the plane is taking off.

10 I really think you *should/shouldn't* call him now. It's already midnight, so he may be asleep.

2 Match sentences 1–7 with responses a)–g).

1 Oh no, there's no milk left!

2 I'm tired today.

3 I've got an exam tomorrow.

4 I broke John's calculator.

5 Lunch is provided.

6 The concert was free.

7 What's the deadline for the report?

a) You must hand it in before 2p.m. on Friday.

b) You should have bought some yesterday.

c) So I don't have to bring food. That's perfect!

d) You should buy him a new one.

e) You mustn't go to bed late.

f) You shouldn't have gone out so late last night.

g) So you didn't have to pay to get in. Fantastic!

3 A How is *have* pronounced in these sentences? Underline it if it is pronounced /əv/. Circle it if it is pronounced /hæf/.

1 I have to leave right now.

2 You should have been more careful.

3 Did you have to pay for parking?

4 We have had to make a few changes.

5 I have got a new car.

6 They don't have to come tomorrow.

B ▶ 3.3 Listen and check. Then listen again and repeat.

READING

4 Which tip, a) b) or c), do you think is the best for each situation? Read the article and check your answers.

1 You worry about taking exams.
   a) Study long hours.   b) Do exercise.

2 You worry about your health.
   a) Talk to your friends.   b) Talk to experts.

3 You worry about your relationships with others.
   a) Try to be like them.   b) Be self-confident.

WHAT DO YOU *WORRY* ABOUT?

Anxiety is a recognised medical issue and as many as one person in three suffers from an anxiety attack at some point in their life. But anxiety isn't always a bad thing; some people actually work better under stress and having to face challenges. However, for other people, worrying makes them physically ill.

Exam worries

Exam anxiety is especially common with students who are academically successful and concerned about their future. If you are one of these people, you often spend your time immersed in books, forgetting that a healthy body leads to a healthy mind. You should make sure you get plenty of rest (no all-night studying just before an exam) and regular exercise. It's important to have breaks and do some physical activity to clear your mind. Drinking too much coffee or overusing other stimulants does not reduce anxiety and may lead to a last minute panic on the exam day.

Good advice?

Health and physical appearance is also a frequent cause of anxiety. In some respects, talking and reading about it can make it worse. For example, you are worried about having headaches. You call up a friend to ask their opinion. They're not an expert and they try to comfort you, but then they tell you about someone they know who had the same symptoms and has a terrible disease! Then, filled with dread, you google the symptoms and you read about all sorts of frightening diagnoses, so you feel twenty times more anxious than when you started. Too much information can be a bad thing when it is not given to you personally by a trained professional.

Social anxiety

Many teenagers and adults worry about what other people think of them. You want to fit in and be liked but trying too hard can stop you feeling comfortable in your own skin. You mustn't worry if some people don't take any notice of you, but just think that they are worse off for not knowing you. You should have confidence in yourself and your own beliefs, but you should also listen to others and try to understand their point of view. It's a combination of tolerance and high self-esteem.

5 Read the article again and underline the correct alternative to complete the sentences.

1 Students who want to do well sometimes spend too much time *panicking/studying*.
2 Exercise helps you to *think more clearly/rest*.
3 Friends' advice isn't always *helpful/truthful*.
4 Good health advice must be *personal/comforting*.
5 You should *respect/question* other people's opinions.

6 Find words/phrases in the article that match definitions 1–8.

1 an uncomfortable feeling of worry (para 1)
   _____
2 completely involved (para 2) _____
3 decrease (para 2) _____
4 illness (para 3) _____
5 fear (para 3) _____
6 confidence in your own abilities (para 4)
   _____

VOCABULARY
LEXICAL CHUNKS: LIFE CHALLENGES

7 Complete sentences 1–6 with phrases a–h.

1 The current economic crisis means that many families find it difficult to ___.
2 Leaving the UK to volunteer in Mexico was a ___. I had no idea what to expect.
3 My son wants to ___ his own business selling sunglasses online.
4 He just wants to ___ with his friends in the shopping mall.
5 I'm not sure I'll be able to ___ all the deliveries on my own. I need someone to help me.
6 She started kickboxing because she wanted to ___ with her friends who did the sport.
7 They didn't ___ the 'No Entry' sign and went into the park.
8 The new volunteers ___ the charity. They are talented and motivated.

a) hang out
b) make ends meet
c) deal with
d) fit in
e) have so much to offer
f) set up
g) take any notice of
h) leap into the unknown

8 Underline the correct alternatives to complete the sentences.

1 When I changed careers and became a schoolteacher, it was a transitional *day/moment*.
2 Even though some people think he's strange, he feels comfortable in his own *place/skin*.
3 When he agreed to take over the business, he was taking a *leap/jump* into the unknown.
4 I tried to ask a question but he didn't *take/make* any notice of me.
5 My sister is really *into/onto* salsa dancing.
6 I was unemployed, so I had to use my savings to make *money/ends* meet.

VOCABULARY PLUS
IDIOMS: RELATIONSHIPS

9 A Match 1–12 with a)–l) to make sentences.

1 My brother and I have a stormy
2 I've never met your other
3 You should give him a second
4 He's only a fair-weather
5 I'm sorry we don't see eye to
6 I need a shoulder to
7 It was truly love at first
8 My mother's one in a
9 We had a meeting to clear the
10 My two friends got on like a house on
11 He's really under the
12 My ex-boyfriend broke my

a) relationship.
b) air.
c) fire.
d) friend.
e) eye.
f) cry on.
g) half.
h) chance.
i) million.
j) thumb.
k) heart.
l) sight.

B Complete the sentences with idioms from Exercise 9A.

1 His donation means the charity will be able to help thousands of children. He's _____.
2 She comes to my parties but she didn't visit when I broke my leg. She's only a _____.
3 My business partner and I don't _____ about how to run the company, so we're always arguing.
4 They met on a blind date and got _____. They enjoy each other's company.
5 Please give me _____. I'll try to improve.
6 My neighbours are shouting again. I think they have a _____ and might separate soon.
7 After the argument we both realised we needed to talk about it again to _____, otherwise we might ruin our friendship.
8 Have you met my _____? We've been together for two years.

VOCABULARY
EVERYDAY ISSUES

1 A Match the adjectives with prefixes 1–7 with their definitions a-g.

1 **un**acceptable
2 **under**estimated
3 **out**dated
4 **over**priced
5 **mis**leading
6 **sub**standard
7 **dis**connected

a) removed, taken away
b) giving a false impression
c) excessively expensive
d) insufficiently calculated
e) too bad to be allowed
f) lower than the minimum quality required
g) old-fashioned

B Complete the email with the adjectives in Exercise 1A.

To   Editor
From   R.Smith

Dear Editor,

It's shocking how the elderly can sometimes be completely abandoned, especially when they live in a big city. A recent apartment fire has brought this issue to the media's attention. Harriet Fallow, a ninety-year-old with no family, couldn't pay her electricity bill, so the supply was ¹_____. The fire started because she used a candle to light her room.

We can find many other cases of elderly people living in ²_____ accommodation, with no washing facilities and ³_____ equipment that is old and dangerous to use. Basic services such as power are ⁴_____, so these people, who have little income, can't afford the minimum comfort such as heating or decent food. The case of Harriet just shows how ⁵_____ government reports are when they claim everyone has access to a reasonable standard of living. In fact, recent surveys have shown that the extent of the problem has been ⁶_____ and is more common than was previously thought. It is ⁷_____ that these people are refused access to essential services.

Yours,

R. Smith

Send

2 Match issues 1–6 with possible solutions a)–f).

1 The information on your company website is outdated.
2 The fish in the supermarket is overpriced.
3 A builder is using substandard cement for the wall he's building.
4 Your water supply has been disconnected.
5 The information in a holiday brochure is misleading.
6 The way an employee dresses is unacceptable.

a) Ask them to change their clothes.
b) Go to a different store.
c) Pay your bill immediately.
d) Redo it with the latest details.
e) Complain to the tourist office.
f) Talk to the architect in charge.

FUNCTION
RESOLVING CONFLICT

3 A ▶ 3.4 Listen and match conversations 1–5 with situations a)–e).

a) two colleagues discussing decorating the office _____
b) a boss and a worker discussing some work _____
c) a shop assistant and customer discussing a purchase _____
d) a husband and wife talking about their weekend plans _____
e) two neighbours in the street talking about a problem _____

B Listen again and complete the sentences from the conversations.

1 a) Good morning. _____ return this hairdryer I bought last month.
  b) _____ speak to the manager about this?
2 a) I'm sorry to bother you, but _____ move your car.
  b) If possible, _____ to park a little further down the street?
3 a) Well, we do need to paint it. _____ another colour?
  b) _____ choose blue?
4 a) Well, I _____ to get the facts right.
  b) _____ go through the points together and I will explain?
5 a) Look, there's something _____ about.
  b) Well, _____ you drive me there, say hello and then go to play golf while we chat?

LEARN TO
SOUND TACTFUL

4 Complete the sentences with the phrases in the box.

I thought maybe	I wonder if	perhaps you could
there's something	the thing is	would you be able

1 _____ to give me the information this week?
2 _____ call him today?
3 _____ I'm rather busy.
4 _____ you had finished the work.
5 _____ you would mind moving your bag?
6 _____ I have to tell you.

VOCABULARY

SCIENCE

1 Match 1–6 with a)–f) to make sentences.

1 The researchers have found tiny organisms
2 We have collected a lot of data
3 It's clear that our findings prove
4 This is the only habitat
5 They have to measure
6 The information is put into a database

a) which is used to classify the data.
b) where these creatures still live in the wild.
c) about the behaviour of chimpanzees.
d) that live on the shells of the turtles.
e) the existence of a new species.
f) the size of the territory.

2 Underline the correct alternatives to complete the sentences.

1 The university has a huge *database/experiment* to store information about the latest research.
2 The doctors *monitored/analysed* his breathing for several days after the accident.
3 They have a lot of *data/organisms* to support their theory.
4 I hope you have *proved/measured* the amount of radioactivity correctly to see if it's safe to be here.
5 I hope to publish my *findings/samples* in a scientific magazine soon.

READING

3 Read the article and choose the best title, a), b) or c).

a) Rebuilding a forest
b) The death of a forest
c) Creating a natural park

4 Read the article again. Are the statements true (T) or false (F)?

1 More than half the forest was destroyed by the cyclone.
2 There were famous trees in Bussaco National Forest.
3 People lived in the forest in the past.
4 Bussaco Digital uses technology to motivate people to help reforestation.
5 People have to visit the forest to see the location of the tree they sponsored.
6 The project has only been supported by businesses.

5 Match the words in bold in the article with definitions 1–5.

1 an understanding of something
2 computer system
3 protection of plants and animals
4 covering a large area
5 amount

On 19 January 2013 Cyclone Gong passed through the Bussaco (Buçaco) National Forest in Portugal. When the storm hit, the wind speeds were high and hundreds of trees were damaged. Once the data was collected, it was estimated that about forty percent of the forest was affected. Some of the most well-known and extraordinary trees had fallen down or had to be cut down due to the damage. The destruction of this ancient collection of trees was **extensive** and when you look at the long history of this 105-hectare site, you realise how important it was to protect it and restore it to how it was before.

The forest's history

The forest has a documented past going back to the sixth century. Initially, it was home to a convent and then a palace (now a hotel) and nowadays it is also a natural habitat to over fifty-six species of animals and visited by many tourists. Unfortunately, as soon as the foundation that manages the forest realised the **extent** of the damage, they knew that they didn't have the money to repair it all themselves. In order to replant all the trees that had been blown down in the storm, a community project called Bussaco Digital was started, combining technology with environmental **awareness**.

Bussaco Digital

The project involved an online **platform** where individuals, companies and schools could choose a species of tree they wanted to plant, from a choice of 250 types. Using GPS coordinates, they could see exactly where that tree had been planted in the forest and even view it on Google Earth. If you wanted to check on your tree, you could visit it and even dedicate it to a loved one. In addition, the fallen trees were used in many different ways: one ancient tree called Cedro de São José, which was brought down in the storm, was used to make a small bridge, and other fallen trees were used to make furniture.

The future

The great benefit of this project is that unless another storm hits the area in the near future, the money raised can continue to be used to improve **conservation** in the area while also supporting educational workshops and the local economy. How successful has the project been? Well, thousands of schools and corporations have planted trees, together with a large number of individuals. It will take time for the forest to recover from the storm, but thanks to this initiative, it is going in the right direction.

GRAMMAR
ZERO, FIRST AND SECOND CONDITIONALS

6 Find and correct the mistakes with tenses in the sentences.

1 If you wouldn't rush your work, you wouldn't make so many mistakes.
2 As soon as I see him, I give him the good news.
3 Would you be interested if I would offer you the job?
4 I don't tell him unless you ask me to do so.
5 If you promise to look after it, I lend you my dress.
6 I love to go on a cruise if I had someone to go.

7 Complete the sentences with the correct form of the verbs in brackets.

1 If she _____ (know) the truth, she wouldn't be happy.
2 When I see your teacher, I _____ (tell) her about the excursion.
3 I _____ (help) you with the boxes if I could, but I've got a bad back.
4 They'll be disappointed if we _____ (not go) to their party.
5 If we don't catch the 10 o'clock train, we _____ (miss) our connection.
6 When the general _____ (give) an order, the soldiers all obey.
7 If my car _____ (be) stolen, I'd go straight to the police.
8 I _____ (often/go) to the gym by the school if I have a free moment.

8 A ▶ 4.1 Listen and tick the sentence you hear, a) or b).

1 a) They'd choose the red one.
　b) They'll choose the red one.
2 a) What would you do?
　b) What will you do?
3 a) I'd make a cake.
　b) I'll make a cake.
4 a) She wouldn't be happy.
　b) She won't be happy.

B Listen again and repeat.

WRITING
A PROPOSAL; LEARN TO USE POSITIVE LANGUAGE

9 Read the proposal below and answer the questions.

1 What is the name of the organisation? _____
2 Who do they want to help? _____
3 What do they want to raise money for? _____
4 What will they use the grant for? _____

---

new save edit　　　　share

Executive summary

Eyes for All would like to ¹**get** a grant of €20,000, to support their campaign to provide e-glasses, a recent technological development, for use by legally blind children and adults.

Organisation information

Eyes for All is a charity that was ²**started** by Jan Donson, whose two teenage children have a condition that causes low vision. There are already over 2,000 registered members of the charity, which is run by a team of three full-time workers.

Goals and objectives

With the development of new technologies, there are real opportunities for people with low vision to be able to see. E-glasses have a high speed, high definition camera which videos what is seen. The e-glasses enhance and improve the images to meet the particular needs of the user. The enhanced video is then played back almost immediately to the user. Our ³**first** aim is to raise funds to buy five pairs of e-glasses to donate to the local Low Vision Centre, to help teenagers and young adults, in particular with their studies.

These amazing devices will allow students to read easily, go to lectures and, probably most importantly for them, be able to see the faces of their friends and colleagues. The long-term ⁴**idea** is to help every person access this technology, even if they can't afford it themselves.

Description of the project

We plan to set up a publicity campaign to encourage donations. This will cover three areas. Firstly, we will organise events, where the money raised will go towards the fund. Secondly, we will create teams of volunteers who will ask for donations on the street. The third and most effective project is to create an online platform which ⁵**tells** the general public about the nature of our work. This will make people more aware of the possibilities that people with low vision have if they ⁶**can** get new technologies. By ⁷**looking** at the number of visits to our site, we will be able to judge the impact we are making.

Budget

€10,000 will be used for ⁸**making** the website and €10,000 will go towards the costs of event production, such as renting venues or printing promotional material like T-shirts for our volunteers. A more detailed breakdown of the costs is attached.

10 Replace the words/phrases in bold in the proposal 1–8 with the more formal words/phrases a)–h).

a) objective
b) apply for
c) will inform
d) have access to
e) monitoring
f) founded
g) developing
h) initial

11 Write a proposal asking your local authority for a grant for a science trip. You want to take a group of children whose families cannot afford to pay for activities outside school. Use the headings in the proposal in Exercise 9 to organise your ideas.

VOCABULARY
REPORTING VERBS

1 A Put the letters in brackets in the correct order to complete the sentences.

1 Politicians _____ (erega) that more money should be invested in the project.

2 Scientists _____ (sgstgeu) that climate change is caused by global warming.

3 Some people _____ (ilmca) that they have met aliens from other planets.

4 Finance experts _____ (proter) that we spend more on our cars than our children.

5 Recent studies _____ (whos) that more people are living alone.

6 The latest findings _____ (opver) that there is water on Mars.

7 Specialists _____ (rimocfn) that back pain can be cured.

8 Most people _____ (elibeve) that technology improves their lives.

B Complete sentence b) so that it has a similar meaning to a). Use the words in Exercise 1A.

1 **a)** You have definitely been nominated for a prize.
   b) I can _____ that you have been nominated for a prize.

2 **a)** The results of the experiment demonstrate that there may be a link between the two species.
   b) The results of the experiment _____ that there may be a link between the two species.

3 **a)** I have evidence that a virus caused the epidemic.
   b) I can _____ that a virus caused the epidemic.

4 **a)** I propose the theory that a meteorite hit the Earth 65 million years ago.
   b) I _____ that a meteorite hit the Earth 65 million years ago.

5 **a)** We all have the same opinion that more research is needed.
   b) We all _____ that more research is needed.

6 **a)** They say that they have found a cure but they have no real evidence.
   b) They _____ that they have found a cure.

7 **a)** Science journals tell us about the latest technological developments.
   b) Science journals _____ the latest technological developments.

8 **a)** They think the drug will save many lives.
   b) They _____ the drug will save many lives.

LISTENING

2 A ▶ 4.2 Listen to four people talking about technology. Match speakers 1–4 with statements a)–d).

1 Emma
3 Isla
2 Philip
4 Denis

a) Technology doesn't improve learning in the classroom. ____

b) Technology is damaging our planet. ____

c) Technology gives disabled people a chance to live a normal life. ____

d) Technology enables people to live and work almost anywhere they want. ____

B Listen again and answer the questions.

1 Who likes to work outside sometimes? ____

2 Who thinks technology doesn't help memory? ____

3 Who uses technology to write? ____

4 Who thinks we are sometimes irresponsible with technology? ____

5 Who uses videoconferencing for their work? ____

6 Who is a student? ____

7 Who feels their job is important? ____

8 Who is worried about the speed of changes in technology? ____

3 Read extracts 1–5 from the recording. Match the words in bold with definitions a)–e).

1 I always had to organise for that person to be there **in advance**.

2 Students are more **eager** to learn on iPads.

3 They are **stationary** all the time.

4 It is **vital** that I keep up to date with the latest medical knowledge.

5 My patients feel more **secure** when they know I have the support of other experts.

a) before a particular time

b) not moving

c) safe

d) keen

e) extremely important

GRAMMAR
PASSIVE REPORTING STRUCTURES

4 Complete the sentences with the correct form of the verbs in brackets.

1 Nowadays it *is thought* (think) that all our children will live to over 100 years old.

2 The cost of the project *is estimated to be* (estimate/be) over 2 million pounds, which is more than we can afford.

3 In the newspaper last week, the planes _____ (report/fly) at speeds of 2,000 km/h.

4 In the past it _____ (believe) that the world was flat.

5 The findings _____ (show/be) wrong when the scientist found a mistake in the calculations.

6 Recently, it _____ (claim) that aliens have visited our planet.

7 The government _____ (say/have) the worst economic policy in decades.

8 It _____ (confirm) that the man has been arrested.

5 Find and correct the mistakes in the sentences.

1 The amount of pesticides in our food is estimating to be increasing.

2 It believed that the discovery will change our lives.

3 The puma was reported be living in the park.

4 The explosion was think to be caused by a gas leak.

5 There is said that we are more stressed these days.

6 It was be confirmed that the paintings were authentic.

7 Young people are thought that less respectful than in the past.

8 It has been agreed to the grant will go to our project.

6 Complete the article with the phrases in the box.

| is estimated   is now suggested   are believed to date |
| is claimed to be   are said to include   are already reported |
| was previously thought   has been agreed to include |

Creative cave people

Following the recent discovery of cave drawings in the west of the country, which ¹_____ back to the Palaeolithic age, archaeologists have called for more funding. The amount of funding necessary ²_____ to be around €100,000, in order to secure the site because the caves ³_____ to be damaged because of curious visitors. The drawings ⁴_____ the most amazing detail and it ⁵_____ that the people who created them had a much more sophisticated understanding of anatomy and perspective than it ⁶_____. This discovery ⁷_____ one of the most significant finds in recent years and it ⁸_____ the site in the World Heritage catalogue.

VOCABULARY PLUS
WORD-BUILDING: COMMONLY CONFUSED WORDS

7 A Underline the correct alternatives to complete the sentences.

1 The *principal/principle* ingredients of the dish are potato and eggs.

2 A good psychologist is *sensible/sensitive* towards the feelings of other people.

3 She's done everything *accept/except* write up the report.

4 He *right/rightly* told the media about the illegal recordings.

5 This car is very *economic/economical* to run. It hardly uses any petrol.

6 You need to buy some *stationary/stationery* before you start your course.

7 I've never had the *possibility/opportunity* to meet a film star.

8 I recommend everyone should *experience/experiment* a day in our spa.

9 The police *advice/advise* people to use public transport during demonstrations.

10 Those green earrings really *complement/compliment* your dress.

B Complete the conversations with the words in italics in Exercise 7A.

A

A: Good morning, doctor. I wonder if you could ¹_____ me about the best way to get fit.

B: Of course. What exercise do you usually do?

A: I don't often have the ²_____ to do much because I'm busy at work.

B: Well, it isn't ³_____ to try and do too much at first – you might hurt yourself. Maybe walking in your lunch hour?

B

A: I need some paper for the printer. I've looked in the ⁴_____ cupboard, but there's none left. Is there any ⁵_____ you could go out and buy some?

B: That's not really my job. Sorry, no one is authorised to purchase stationery ⁶_____ Jackie in the admin team.

C

A: Your final project was excellent, Paula. You are one of my best students.

B: Thanks for the ⁷_____! I'm delighted with my results.

A: What are your plans now?

B: I hope to get some ⁸_____ as an intern with a company this summer. Then I may do a Master's.

VOCABULARY
INTERNET WORDS/PHRASES

1 Underline the correct alternatives to complete the sentences.

1 If you join a lot of networking sites, you'll have a more extensive digital *footprint/market/account*.

2 He sent me a *view/setup/screenshot* of the login page to show me the problem he was having.

3 Businesses commonly use social *media/profiles/research* to advertise their services.

4 Some search *motors/engines/lookers* are better than others for finding information.

5 He posted horrible messages on her blog, so she accused him of *cyberbullying/cyber offence/cyber attack*.

6 All you have to do is *post/test/google* his name and he appears at the top of the list.

7 You can buy good quality shoes online at the click of a(n) *finger/button/eye*.

8 I had to set up a new email *number/account/site* when my old one was hacked.

9 After two weeks the file transfer service will *find/delete/search* the documents you uploaded.

10 The program will install the latest *media/screens/updates* when you connect to the internet.

FUNCTION
HEDGING

2 A Read the conversations. Why is Speaker B hedging? Match conversations 1–4 with reasons a)–d).

1 **A:** So what have you been doing these days, Dave?
B: Oh, nothing particularly. Just keeping busy.
A: Come on! The last I heard you'd started a business.
B: Maybe I've done something like that.

2 **A:** So, Matt, what are the results of the research so far?
B: Well, I guess we've made some progress.
A: Can you be a little more precise?
B: Umm … it's kind of going well, but I'm not sure of the exact figures.
A: Have you actually prepared any of the information for this meeting, Matt?

3 **A:** So, Jon, what did you think of the concert last night?
B: Oh I didn't really enjoy it.
A: What do you mean? It was great!
B: Well, I suppose it was OK, but I think the band are possibly a bit past their best.
A: Come on! They're classics!
B: You could say that.

4 **A:** What did you do with the scissors, Kevin?
B: Presumably, I left them in the kitchen drawer.
A: No, I've looked there. You had them yesterday.
B: Maybe I put them in the cupboard or something.
A: You're useless. Come and help me find them!

The speaker:
a) doesn't know the answer.
b) doesn't want to give away information.
c) can't remember.
d) wants to be polite but disagrees.

B Read the conversations in Exercise 2A again. Underline the words/phrases which show that Speaker B is hedging.

3 Match questions 1–6 with responses a)–f).

1 How much did you pay for that old car?
2 Did you enjoy your meal?
3 Have you finished your homework?
4 Why did you give him money?
5 When does the series start?
6 Who is he texting?

a) A friend or someone.
b) Not much, really.
c) I just thought he needed it.
d) I suppose it was alright.
e) The same time as always, presumably.
f) I've kind of done my maths.

LEARN TO
USE HESITATION DEVICES

4 A ▶ 4.3 Listen to Steve introducing himself to colleagues on a course. How many times does he hesitate?

B Listen again and complete the sentences with the hesitation devices Steve uses.

1 I've been working for, _____ … nearly ten years as a computer programmer.

2 What do I like to do in my free time? _____, I don't like sport much. _____, I don't go to the gym or anything like that.

3 I really like making models. _____, models that really work.

4 I suppose it sounds a bit childish, but _____, it's actually quite technical, so it's challenging.

GRAMMAR NARRATIVE TENSES

1 Find and correct the mistakes in the sentences.

1 He was seeing the accident when he was walking home from work.
2 She had nearly finished eating her salad when she had seen the insect on her plate.
3 She took a photo of him when he didn't look.
4 I wasn't knowing that you were in the bathroom.
5 Before he can react, the man had taken his phone.
6 I was falling while I was getting out of the shower.
7 I opened the curtains and saw the sun shone.
8 By the time he got to the party, everyone went home.

VOCABULARY ADVERBS

2 Underline the correct alternatives to complete the sentences.

1 What can we *realistically/literally/typically* do, given that we only have limited resources?
2 The soldiers bravely *ran away from/fought against/looked at* the huge invading army.
3 I *literally/desperately/amazingly* need some new shoes. Mine have holes in them!
4 She's had a lot of visitors in hospital. Her room is *cheerfully/bravely/literally* full of cards.
5 He was *bravely/realistically/amazingly* lucky to escape with his life in the accident.
6 It was a lovely day and he sang *undoubtedly/cheerfully/realistically* to himself as he walked along the street.

GRAMMAR MODELS OF OBLIGATION – PRESENT/PAST

3 Complete the conversation with the phrases in the box.

must say   mustn't stop   didn't have to look
don't have to worry   had to give   have to answer
have to find   should apply   should have prepared
should think

A: How did the interview go, Jane?
B: Well, I ¹_____ I was disappointed.
A: Why's that?
B: Well, I wore a suit and the boss was wearing jeans!
A: So you ²_____ formal?
B: No, I felt a bit embarrassed. Anyway, I ³_____ a presentation and answer questions.
A: Did you ⁴_____ any difficult questions?
B: Yes, and I ⁵_____ more.
A: Why?
B: Because I didn't know what to say.
A: Well, next time you ⁶_____ about what they'll ask.
B: Yes, I realise that I ⁷_____ so much about my appearance but I ⁸_____ out more about the company.
A: Well, you ⁹_____ trying. You ¹⁰_____ for more jobs and learn from the experience.
B: You're right.

LEXICAL CHUNKS LIFE CHALLENGES

4 Replace the words in bold in the sentences with the words/phrases in the box.

is comfortable in his own skin   is into
take a leap into the unknown
set up   take any notice of   dread
transitional moment   hang out
make ends meet   deal with

1 The receptionist just couldn't **handle** all the calls about the new product.
2 I've got five children so even with a good salary, it's not easy to **pay for everything we need**.
3 He had to **try something he hadn't done before** when he took on the new job.
4 **I'm afraid of** going to the dentist.
5 He **enjoys seeing** live football matches and goes every weekend.
6 He doesn't **pay attention to** me when I ask a question.
7 He **feels happy with the way he is** and has no intention of changing.
8 This is a **time of change** for our country.
9 They've decided to **start** a new business.
10 Teenagers just like to **spend time** with their friends at weekends.

VOCABULARY PLUS IDIOMS: RELATIONSHIPS

5 Complete the words in the letter. The first letter of each word is given.

Dear Ellen,
I'm writing to you about a problem I have.
As you know, I have been living with Sue, my other ¹h_____, for two years but nowadays we're having a ²s_____ relationship, arguing and fighting about everything. We used to get on like a ³h_____ on fire but now I feel like she wants me under her ⁴t_____ and doesn't let me make my own decisions. I thought she was one in a ⁵m_____ and the only one for me. When we met, it was love at first ⁶s_____ but now we can't seem to clear the ⁷a_____ after we have had an argument. She never gives me a ⁸s_____ chance if I do something wrong. I really need a ⁹s_____ to cry on, but all our friends know both of us, so it's difficult. You are the only person I can talk to. Please give me some advice! Should I leave her?

VOCABULARY EVERYDAY ISSUES

6 Add a prefix from box A to the words in box B to complete the sentences.

A
dis- mis- out- over- sub- un- under-

B
priced dated acceptable cooked due
connected leading standard

1 The journalist wrote a(n) _____ article about the funding for the project, saying it was illegal when we had approval from the government.
2 I find his behaviour completely _____ and I won't tolerate his presence in my house.
3 The router has been _____, so we can't get wi-fi in the building.
4 I was ill because the chicken had been _____, which is quite dangerous, actually.
5 I think electric cars are totally _____, so I'm going to wait a couple of years before I buy one.
6 The imitation watches are _____, so they don't work properly.
7 The baby is a week _____, so the pregnant woman will have to go to hospital immediately.
8 That textbook is _____ and mentions nothing about recent political changes.

FUNCTION RESOLVING CONFLICT

7 Underline the correct alternatives to complete the conversations.

1
A: ¹Can/Shall I talk to you about something?
B: Sure. What's the problem?
A: Well, you know that red suit you've got?
B: Yes, what about it?
A: The thing ²says/is, the boss thinks it looks too bright.
B: Really? I never knew.
A: ³Because/Perhaps you could just wear it at weekends.

2
A: Terry, there's something I ⁴would/need to talk to you about.
B: Yeah, what?
A: The problem ⁵is/was that you never do your share of housework.
B: Well, you know I don't have time.
A: But it's ⁶making/having it impossible for me to find time to study.
B: I suppose you're right. ⁷What if/Why not you clean and I'll deal with the clothes?
A: That's a start!

VOCABULARY SCIENCE

8 Complete the extract from a report with the words in the box.

organisms examine analyse data database
habitat monitor samples findings measure

Introduction

This report summarises the ¹_____ and conclusions from our research into the marine ²_____ of shellfish that are native to the North Sea coast of Scotland. We set out to prove that the recent increase in shipping traffic in the area has affected the population of these creatures due to pollution. This pollution has had a negative impact on the ³_____ that they feed on. We decided to ⁴_____ water ⁵_____ taken from different depths and ⁶_____ the amount of toxic substances in them. This ⁷_____, together with figures on shellfish numbers, was included in a(n) ⁸_____. In order to ⁹_____ changes in the use of the new port area, the authorities let us ¹⁰_____ the daily schedules and we compared this information with the fluctuations in the shellfish population.

GRAMMAR ZERO, FIRST AND SECOND CONDITIONALS

9 Complete the sentences with the words in the box.

is (x2) won't be won't come have had
will have don't have (x2) feels would feel
lose lost get wouldn't get will find find
didn't work don't work wouldn't work

1 He _____ a lot better if he _____ some weight.
2 It _____ impossible to climb the mountain if you _____ oxygen.
3 Unless the rabbit _____ safe, it _____ out of its hole.
4 If you _____ your key, there _____ an extra one under the flowerpot.
5 When the children _____ lunch, they _____ well in the afternoon.
6 If I _____ the choice, I _____ in an office.
7 As soon as you _____ home, you _____ me cooking in the kitchen.
8 I _____ able to concentrate unless I _____ complete silence.
9 If you _____ so hard, you _____ so stressed.
10 Unless I _____ my wallet, I _____ to cancel my credit cards.

VOCABULARY REPORTING VERBS

10 Look at the reporting verbs in bold and match sentences 1–6 with sentences a–f.

1 Biologists **agree** that the problem is serious.
2 The ecologists **claim** that the factory is dumping chemicals in the river.
3 The results **prove** the existence of life on the planet.
4 Studies **show** that younger children learn more quickly.
5 The media **report** that there has been seismic activity in the area.
6 Scientists **believe** global warming can be stopped.

a) They have the opinion it is true.
b) They say it is true but without concrete proof.
c) They have the same opinion.
d) They tell us about it.
e) They give definite evidence that it is true.
f) They demonstrate a fact.

GRAMMAR PASSIVE REPORTING STRUCTURES

11 Rewrite each sentence in two ways.

1 People claim that the temperature is rising.
It _____ that the temperature is rising.
The temperature _____ rising.
2 Scientists have shown that smog causes cancer.
It _____ that smog causes cancer.
Smog _____ cancer.
3 Experts agreed that the paintings were imitations.
It _____ that the paintings were imitations.
The paintings _____ only imitations.
4 The police think that three people took part in the robbery.
It _____ that three people took part in the robbery.
Three people _____ part in the robbery.

VOCABULARY PLUS COMMONLY CONFUSED WORDS

12 Find and correct the mistakes in the sentences. Five sentences are correct.

1 The principal issue is where to get the money for the rebuilding, not the design.
2 She's very sensible to other people's feelings and always knows what to say.
3 You should buy a scarf that complements your shirt.
4 The new supermarket sells clothes that are very economic, so I've already bought a cheap skirt there.
5 As you rightly say, we need to do something about this.
6 Can you give me another possibility to improve the report?
7 People have experimented strange phenomena in the castle.
8 As she turned the corner, she crashed into a stationary van.
9 He finds it hard to except that he's getting older.
10 You've given me some good advice over the years.

VOCABULARY WORDS /PHRASES

13 Complete the sentences with the words in the box.

profile	click	google	delete
footprint	search	screenshot	
cyberbullying	social	post	

1 To access the site, all you have to do is _____ on the button that says 'Enter'.
2 There are very few people in this country who don't leave a digital _____ somewhere on the web.
3 She didn't want the school to _____ photos of her children online.
4 I took a _____ of the webpage to use in my presentation.
5 The problem of _____ is increasing as more people write unpleasant anonymous messages online.
6 I managed to _____ those embarrassing photos of myself but I worry that someone else has kept a copy.
7 I always use the same _____ engine to look for shopping websites.
8 You can waste a lot of time on _____ media sites as they encourage you to read a lot of useless information.
9 I need to update my _____ on LinkedIn now that I have been promoted.
10 I often _____ names of old friends to see if I can find out where they are.

FUNCTION HEDGING

14 Underline the words/phrases that make the sentences less direct.

1 She's not particularly keen on Chinese food.
2 I suppose you can borrow my car.
3 He gave me a kind of strange present.
4 It's maybe something he'd want to do.
5 He just wanted to help.
6 I need a pencil or something to do the crossword.
7 They aren't really able to deal with the situation.
8 You might have made a mistake.

CHECK

Circle the correct answer, a), b) or c), to complete the sentences.

1 We _____ in the queue when it started to rain.
   a) had waited   **b)** were waiting   **c)** waited

2 I _____ the article before my sister told me about it.
   a) had seen   **b)** was seeing   **c)** see

3 They noticed that _____ hundreds of people were leaving the city.
   a) amazingly   **b)** bravely   **c)** literally

4 He is _____ the best new singer this year.
   a) undoubtedly   **b)** cheerfully   **c)** desperately

5 _____ nobody thought she could do it, she managed to finish the marathon.
   a) Although   **b)** Despite   **c)** Besides

6 The invitation says it's an informal party, so you _____ wear a suit.
   a) mustn't   **b)** don't have to   **c)** shouldn't

7 I knew that I _____ earlier when I saw the traffic jam in front of me.
   a) should have left   **b)** must leave   **c)** had to leave

8 They _____ so much food. We've got plenty here.
   a) should have brought   **b)** must bring
   c) didn't have to bring

9 My boss didn't _____ any notice of my request.
   a) take   **b)** make   **c)** pay

10 How can you deal _____ so many refugees?
    a) of   **b)** with   **c)** for

11 She won't help me now I'm ill. She's a _____ friend.
    a) fair-weather   **b)** stormy   **c)** second

12 The evening we met we _____ like a house on fire.
    a) talked   **b)** argued   **c)** got on

13 The _____ service in that restaurant is because they don't have enough staff.
    a) substandard   **b)** misleading   **c)** outdated

14 I _____ if you could show me how to use the photocopier.
    a) want   **b)** wonder   **c)** would like

15 I've got _____ I need to talk to you about.
    a) anything   **b)** something   **c)** thing

16 You have to _____ a blood sample to test for infection.
    a) monitor   **b)** take   **c)** prove

17 The latest _____ indicate that the ancient civilisation used wooden houses.
    a) findings   **b)** habitats   **c)** tools

18 If you felt worried about something, who _____ you talk to?
    a) will   **b)** would   **c)** do

19 This country would be at war _____ we didn't have a strong leader.
    a) if   **b)** whether   **c)** unless

20 Unless you _____ better, you won't be invited again.
    a) don't behave   **b)** behaved   **c)** behave

21 If the garden _____ bigger, I could plant more flowers.
    a) is   **b)** would be   **c)** were

22 I was on the train with my colleagues at that time, so I can _____ that I wasn't at the crime scene.
    a) agree   **b)** prove   **c)** claim

23 Many scientists don't _____ that the new drug will cure malaria.
    a) believe   **b)** confirm   **c)** report

24 It has been _____ that the president is going to resign.
    a) confirm   **b)** confirms   **c)** confirmed

25 The boys _____ talented players.
    a) are said to be   **b)** are said that   **c)** are said be

26 He bought everyone a drink _____ his brother, who already had one.
    a) accept   **b)** except   **c)** apart

27 These are very _____ cars. Shall we buy one?
    a) economics   **b)** economic   **c)** economical

28 I haven't put my _____ picture on the webpage.
    a) profile   **b)** account   **c)** place

29 I have joined three social _____ sites in the past year.
    a) engine   **b)** email   **c)** media

30 I'm not sure but think I got an email about the changes to my bank account _____.
    a) particularly   **b)** or something   **c)** kind of

RESULT   /30

5)) EXPLORE

VOCABULARY

NATURE

1 Complete the text with the words in the box.

> vegetation   parasites   creatures   diseases
> floods   canopy   snakes   rainforest

Survival tours

- Join our Amazon adventure trip. Spend five days in the northern Amazon ¹_____ learning how to survive in the jungle. You'll have the opportunity to climb to the top of a sixty-metre tall tree and be amazed by the views over the ²_____ of trees.

- Our expert guides will inform you about the jungle ³_____ you see, helping you to identify venomous ⁴_____ or edible insects. You will learn how to use plants and fruit found in the thick ⁵_____ on the jungle floor. Survival skills also include protecting yourself from illness. You learn about ⁶_____ like worms that can get under your skin, and how to remove them and also how local people use natural medicine to fight ⁷_____.

- This tour is not available in the rainy season because of the danger of flash ⁸_____ in the area.

LISTENING

2 A ▶ 5.1 Listen to Nick and Helen discussing why they use a map app. Tick the reasons they talk about.
1 to find the way to a destination
2 to plan a walking route
3 to look at a place they are going to visit
4 to calculate the distance between places
5 to observe unusual places

B Listen again. Are the statements true (T) or false (F)?
1 Helen knows people who appear on Google Maps Street View.
2 Nick likes to view his holiday destinations using a map application.
3 You can see an accurate picture of the White House on Google Maps.
4 The Faroe Islands are blacked out on Google Earth.
5 Nick thinks that the black areas on the map hide secret places.
6 It's free to pixelate the image of your home on Google Maps.
7 Sandy Island was declared to be non-existent in 2012.

3 Read extracts 1–7 from the recording. Match the words in bold with definitions a)–g).
1 I've seen a few funny shots of people wearing masks or doing something **weird**.
2 We think these maps **document** everywhere in the world.
3 A large section of the area is **blurred**.
4 This was to **prevent** terrorists or others using the map to plan attacks.
5 It looks like someone has **pasted** images on top of others.
6 Important people ask Google to pixelate their homes for reasons of **privacy**.
7 You can still find its **imaginary** position marked.

a) put, stuck
b) stop
c) strange
d) record, verify

e) the right to keep your life secret
f) not real
g) not clear

GRAMMAR

QUANTIFIERS

4 Underline the correct alternatives to complete the sentences.
1 We only had a *few/little* money left after our holiday.
2 *A great deal/A large number* of people took part in the demonstration.
3 There weren't *much/many* things to buy in that shop.
4 They were overwhelmed by the *amount/number* of applications for the job.
5 There are very *little/few* undiscovered places in Europe today.
6 You should get a *few/little* more practice before you take your exam.
7 With a *bit/few* of luck, we'll get there on time.
8 He doesn't have *much/many* work at the moment.
9 I noticed *several/a great deal of* mistakes in the article.
10 Can I ask you a *couple/lot* of questions? I promise it won't take long.

5 Complete the sentences with the words/phrases in the box.

| loads of | bit | couple | little | a little | few |
| a few | much | | | | |

1 I have very _____ information, so I'm afraid I can't help you.
2 I have _____ time to meet you tomorrow. Would 11a.m. be OK?
3 Unfortunately, _____ children are interested in reading nowadays.
4 He doesn't have _____ experience in the field of marketing.
5 The soup needs a(n) _____ of salt.
6 There are _____ apples on the tree, but not many.
7 I last saw Gary a(n) _____ of weeks ago.
8 She spends _____ money on clothes.

6 ▶ 5.2 Underline the words that include the sound /ə/ in connected speech. Listen and check.

1 He gave a few of us maths classes.
2 We got loads of replies.
3 She had a lot of cats.
4 I said a couple of words.

WRITING

A SHORT BOOK REVIEW; LEARN TO OFFER PRAISE AND CRITICISM

7 Underline the correct alternatives to complete the sentences.

1 The autobiography was written by *world-famous/well-researched* Formula One racing driver Graham Hill.
2 The writing style is very *old-fashioned/badly-researched*, so it has little appeal for teenagers.
3 Readers will be convinced by the *compelling/dull* arguments against modern business practices.
4 Although the action is sometimes *well-written/slow-moving*, the city is beautifully described.
5 We are left with a *powerful/charming* image of the tragic consequences of war.
6 The ending of the story was *persuasive/unconvincing* as the murderer was never found.
7 The constant changes from the past to the present made the plot very *difficult/original* to follow.
8 I found the scene of the two abandoned brothers so *persuasive/moving* that I nearly cried as I was reading.

8 Read the review of the book *The Miniaturist*. What does the miniaturist make?

The Miniaturist

by Jessie Burton

Jessie Burton, a British writer who studied at Oxford University and the Central School of Speech and Drama, ¹_____. *The Miniaturist* is her debut novel, written on a creative writing course. The book has been published in thirty-eight languages and it has sold over a million copies.

Set in Amsterdam in the seventeenth century, the novel was inspired by Petronella Oortman's dollhouse in the Rijksmuseum. All the pieces inside this perfect replica of a house were made of the same materials as the real objects, in exactly the right proportions. This fictional story follows the creation of a dollhouse and the mystery of how the maker of the miniature furniture and dolls seems to know intimate details about the family. Incredibly atmospheric, the book ²_____, but most significantly, the role of women in the home at the time.

The book has been written for adults, but ³_____ and has also been made into a drama for the BBC. It is dark and mysterious and, at the heart of the book is the sensation of dread when the characters realise the power of the miniaturist – the shadowy figure who makes the tiny pieces for the dollhouse.

I would recommend this book to anyone who enjoys intrigue and psychology. It is totally absorbing and, like any good thriller, it ⁴_____. It beautifully portrays Amsterdam at that time, with vivid descriptions and a view of the realities of daily life. The main female character, Nella, ⁵_____ because she is probably a bit too modern in her way of thinking, but in the end the reader wants her to succeed.

9 Complete the review in Exercise 8 with phrases a)–e).

a) explores the themes of feeling out of place and loneliness
b) is a little unconvincing
c) is also accessible to teenage readers
d) is both an author and an actor
e) has an unexpected ending

10 Write a short review (200–250 words) of a book you enjoyed. Include information about the author, the audience, the argument (main themes) and your assessment of the book.

VOCABULARY

TYPES OF PEOPLE

1 Match people 1–8 with sentences a)–h).

1	bookworm	**5**	couch potato
2	computer nerd	**6**	foodie
3	beach bum	**7**	news junkie
4	rebellious teenager	**8**	sports fan

a) He refuses to do what his mother asks.

b) She loves reading recipe books and trying out new restaurants.

c) He spends all day surfing and when he's not in the water, he sits around chatting to friends.

d) He watches the 10 o'clock report on one channel, then switches to another for the 11 o'clock bulletin. He also reads two online papers.

e) She likes almost every genre, but historical novels are her favourite. Her mum sometimes worries about her eyesight.

f) He spends all day in front of a screen, programming.

g) She gets home from school and straightaway she's on the sofa with the TV on, eating snacks. I can't get her to do anything else.

h) He can tell you who won the European Cup in 1988, who is the new badminton champion or even the names of the players in the women's hockey team.

READING

2 Read the texts and match photos 1–4 with paragraphs A–D.

3 Read the texts again and answer the questions.

Which person/people (A, B, C or D):

1 doesn't often have the chance to live her perfect day? _____

2 would probably like to change her normal routine? _____ , _____

3 makes friends when she's enjoying herself? _____

4 sometimes does things her parents don't like? _____ , _____

5 doesn't like some aspects of her work? _____

6 enjoys team work? _____

7 is very active? _____

8 likes to be indoors? _____ , _____

9 enjoys cultural activities? _____ , _____

10 likes to be alone? _____

MY PERFECT DAY

My perfect day would be to spend all day gaming with my online community. People seem to think it's lonely being me, but I have a **wider range** of friends, some of whom are techies, some who are more 'normal', than most people I know. We have a lot in common and tend to share ideas and exchange secrets about how to get to the next level or when a new version of a game has been **released**. I meet new people all the time and I think we learn a lot of good values as we often need to work together to score a goal or help each other improve. My mum complains that I don't go out and meet people, but at least she always knows where I am!

A _____

Strangely, my perfect day would involve being at work. I'm surrounded by books and share many of those hidden stories and fascinating facts with customers. I love the smell of books, the **rustle** of pages as you turn them and the way they give readers the chance to imagine a completely different world. The peace and quiet of the place is something you can't find anywhere else, although it's true I would prefer to spend the day **wandering** round the different sections and looking through the new additions rather than checking books in and out.

B _____

Every day my two little girls wake me up at **the crack of dawn**. So, I suppose my perfect day would be any day where I'm allowed to sleep past 6a.m.! But if I had to choose, first I'd have a leisurely breakfast while listening to the radio, followed by a walk around town, just window shopping. As I'm surrounded by kids and staff members all day at work as well, I wouldn't choose to see anyone that day. Maybe I'd eat a sandwich in the park and then, in the afternoon, I'd probably go to the cinema and I'd choose to watch something quite arty, like an old black and white movie.

C _____

In my case, my perfect day would definitely be spent outdoors. I live near the sea and although some people might call me a beach bum, I'd call myself a sports enthusiast. I don't just sit on the beach – actually, I can't stand sitting **still**. I surf, I love to play beach volleyball and I never **miss** a tournament. So, perhaps I'd get up with the sun, get down to the sand and spend the day there with friends. My parents aren't always keen on the amount of time I spend out of the house, but it could be worse: I could be spending all my time on my computer!

D _____

4 Look at the words/phrases in bold in the texts. Underline the correct alternatives to complete the definitions.

1 wider range: more *varied/limited*
2 released: *made available for the public/produced for testing*
3 rustle: a *soft/loud* sound
4 wandering: *thinking/walking* in a relaxed way
5 the crack of dawn: very *late/early*
6 still: without *moving/talking*
7 miss: *lose/not attend*

GRAMMAR

-ING FORM AND INFINITIVE

5 Underline the correct alternatives to complete the sentences.

1 I'm looking forward to *meeting/meet* your cousin.
2 Now I've left home, I really miss *to chat/chatting* to my parents at meal times.
3 They agreed *to finance/financing* the new magazine.
4 We bought a cheap camera *to take/taking* photos underwater.
5 She promised *to not ask/not to ask* any questions.
6 They used the GPS *to find/finding* the hotel.
7 Can you imagine not *having/to have* access to internet for a week?
8 I gave up *having/to have* sugar in my coffee years ago.

6 Complete the sentences with the correct form of the verbs in brackets.

1 Do you fancy _____ (eat) out tonight?
2 He refused _____ (speak) to the police.
3 She apologised to her friend _____ (clear) the air after their argument.
4 She's interested in _____ (go) abroad to study.
5 The cat managed _____ (climb) in through the window.
6 I wish _____ (inform) you of the changes we have planned.
7 My boyfriend doesn't mind _____ (wait) for me after work.
8 My cousins enjoy _____ (spend) time together.

7 Find and correct the mistakes in the sentences. Two sentences are correct.

1 Play tennis is something I only do in the summer.
2 Can you imagine being lost in those mountains?
3 The school decided giving us a day's holiday.
4 They went out for celebrating his birthday.
5 He isn't keen on have friends to stay at his house.
6 We look forward to hearing from you soon.
7 She's sometimes expected working on Saturdays.
8 The best thing about to do sport is the way you feel afterwards.

VOCABULARY PLUS

FORMAL VS INFORMAL REGISTER

8 A Replace the words/phrases in bold in the sentences with the words/phrases in the box.

try-hard chatty hacked off slob fit go-getter hassle loaded veg out chill

1 When he lost his job, he was really **annoyed and upset**.
2 She can start a conversation with anyone. She's so **into talking**.
3 They've got a huge house and two sports cars. They must be **very rich**!
4 I'm exhausted. All I want to do is go home and **sit in front of the telly doing nothing**.
5 His shirt isn't clean and his desk is covered in empty cola cans. He's such a **lazy person**.
6 She's a **very ambitious person** and wants to be a manager by the time she's twenty-five.
7 I have to get a train and two buses to get to work. It's a real **struggle**.
8 She's a **person who tries to impress others too much**, so she's always talking about her great salary.
9 Can't you just **relax** a little and stop worrying?
10 The man in the perfume advert is really **attractive**.

B Complete the sentences with the words/phrases in the box in Exercise 8A.

1 It was a real _____ trying to get here because all the bus drivers are on strike.
2 Even if the interview went badly, you can't do anything about it now, so _____ and talk to me about something else.
3 She's a _____. She leaves her clothes on the floor and never clears up in the kitchen.
4 He's in his fifties, but he's got all these younger friends, so he's bought a sports car and dyed his hair. He's such a _____.
5 It's so boring. All he wants to do at the weekend is _____ and watch sport on TV.
6 My new neighbour is very _____. In fact, she never stops talking!
7 She was totally _____ when she found someone had stolen her phone.
8 I can't afford to go on a safari. I'm not _____, you know.
9 The new manager is really _____. I love those tall dark-haired types!
10 Jack is determined to get a promotion. He's a _____.

VOCABULARY

SOCIETY

1 Complete the conversation with the words in the box.

> housing   unemployment   sanitation   healthcare
> network   media   evasion   poverty

A: Have you seen the news? The ¹_____ figures have gone up. There are now 2 million people without jobs. And the government is cutting the ²_____ budget, so we'll have to wait longer to get an appointment with the doctor.

B: Well, it's not as bad as some other countries, where there is real ³_____. You know, where people have no money and children are dying of hunger.

A: I suppose we do have enough to eat and decent ⁴_____ so we don't have diseases like cholera. But I can't stand the corruption here. Another politician has been accused of tax ⁵_____. I don't know why he can't pay like the rest of us!

B: You're right. And did you see the report on the latest ⁶_____ situation? There aren't enough houses for people living in the city but they can't build outside the metropolitan area because they haven't got the rail ⁷_____ to enable everyone to get to work.

A: They never seem to plan in advance! What's more, the ⁸_____ manipulate the information according to the political party they support, so I never know who to believe.

B: I know. Perhaps you shouldn't watch TV anymore!

2 Match descriptions 1–6 with issues a)–h). There are two extra issues.

1 Even though we live in a developed country, there are still families who cannot afford to feed their children. Schools are providing free meals in these cases but we also need to look at their housing situation.

2 Several blogs and websites have been blocked and people who want to make their voice heard have to use illegal means. There have also been arrests of those who openly criticised the government.

3 Security has been increased in airports, stations and public buildings after the recent events and the government has called on citizens to immediately report anything suspicious they might see.

4 The project involves creating a filter which can be manufactured cheaply, providing a sustainable solution to the problem of diseases caused by bacteria in the untreated water supply.

5 This crime affects everyone. If the authorities don't have money to provide essential services, then we all suffer and it is unfair that some people cheat the system.

6 Since the factory closed, the job situation has become critical in the area. Many young people are leaving to find work in other places and those who cannot because they have family commitments are struggling to make ends meet.

a) child poverty
b) unemployment
c) terrorist threats
d) access to sanitation and clean water
e) freedom of speech
f) tax evasion
g) power cuts
h) healthcare

FUNCTION

EXPRESSING YOUR OPINION

3 A ▶ 5.3 Listen and match conversations 1–6 with photos A–F.

B Complete the words in the extracts from the recording. The first letter of each word is given. Listen again and check your answers.

1 **A:** Yes, but I'm not c_____ that's the best solution. I think they should improve the public transport.
   B: That's a good p_____.

2 **A:** What s_____ we do about all this vandalism?
   B: I s_____ they should put security cameras in.

3 **A:** If you a_____ me, people who drop litter should be fined.
   B: You may be r_____.

4 **B:** Shouldn't s_____ give him a blanket?
   A: It s_____ to me they should provide more homeless shelters.

5 **A:** They've increased security at the station.
   B: As I s_____ it, that won't stop terrorists. They only check suitcases.
   A: T_____ a fair point.

6 **A:** I f_____ that there are more important issues than worrying about animals.
   B: I'm not s_____ about that. We have to protect nature.

LISTENING

1 A ▶ 6.1 **Listen to a radio programme and match people 1–4) with actions a)–d).**

1 Jeff Rochford	a) helped children in need
2 Jamal Rutledge	b) used children for experiments
3 Hell's Angels	c) gave up a criminal life
4 Jonas Salk	d) saved a policeman

B Listen again and circle the correct answer, a), b) or c).

1 What was Jeff doing when he saw the emergency?
   a) robbing a house
   b) cleaning windows
   c) turning into the street
2 What are Jeff's plans for the future?
   a) to help people change their lives
   b) to join the emergency service
   c) to become an athlete
3 Why were people surprised by Jamal Rutledge's actions?
   a) He captured a criminal.
   b) He helped a colleague.
   c) He didn't try to escape.
4 What did the Hell's Angels do to help children?
   a) They gave to a charity.
   b) They bought them motorbikes.
   c) They treated them gently.
5 What was Jonas Salk famous for?
   a) working hard
   b) helping children
   c) medical discoveries

Hell's Angels

2 A Match words 1–5 from the recording with definitions a)–e).

1 behaved	3 inspired	5 separate
2 cases	4 reconcile	

a) get/stay away from
b) acted
c) gave (someone) the good idea (to do something)
d) examples
e) make opposite ideas consistent with each other

B Complete the presenter's comments with the words in Exercise 3A. Listen again and check your answers.

1 Perhaps the praise he was given _____ him to do even more good work.
2 These were individuals who _____ in an admirable way.
3 Do people need to _____ themselves from bad influence?
4 How can people _____ robbery and violence on one hand, and acts of kindness on the other?
5 There are plenty of _____ where the good are bad and the bad are good.

GRAMMAR
MODALS OF DEDUCTION

3 Match sentences 1–8 with sentences a)–h).

1 He should know the answer.
2 He won't come in to the office today.
3 He shan't drink alcohol at the party.
4 He can't be away today as well.
5 He shouldn't get angry.
6 He must be at home tonight.
7 He could be in the mountains today.
8 He won't be late.

a) The meeting has been put off till tomorrow.
b) He's got to drive home.
c) He's always punctual.
d) He never goes out in the evenings.
e) He was on holiday last week.
f) He enjoys hiking.
g) He's really well-informed.
h) He understands the difficulties we've had.

4 Underline the correct alternatives to complete the sentences.

1 I'm not sure where she is, but she *might/can* be in the bathroom.
2 Don't forget the map or you *should/'ll* get lost.
3 They've been working since 5a.m., so they *must/ shouldn't* be exhausted.
4 He said that was Tim's wife, but that *can't/mustn't* be right – Tim's not married.
5 The National Museum *may not/could* be interesting, but I'd prefer to see the main square.
6 I *shan't/shouldn't* tell anyone, I promise.
7 I reckon they *should/won't* be here at about 10 o'clock if they catch the 9.15 train.
8 He always gets up early, so he *won't/might* be annoyed if you phone him at 8.30.
9 Her story *may/must* be true, but I have my doubts.
10 Why is he wearing such a smart suit? *Could/Won't* he be going for a job interview?

VOCABULARY
EXTREME ADJECTIVES

5 Read the clues and complete the crossword.

Across	Down
1 very beautiful	**2** very hungry
3 very crowded	**4** very ugly
6 very big	**5** very old
7 very cold	**7** very dirty
8 very clean	

6 Complete the sentences with the words in the box.

> spotless   ancient   packed   gigantic   hideous
> astonished   starving   filthy   terrifying   gorgeous

1 Tommy, your hands are _____ after playing in the garden! Go and wash them before you eat.
2 The island was almost destroyed by the _____ wave from the tsunami.
3 That orange dress with big pink flowers on it is _____. I don't know how she can wear it!
4 I missed lunch today, so now I'm _____.
5 I hate horror films. I find them _____ and I don't like being scared.
6 When you run a restaurant, the tablecloths and napkins need to be _____ or the customers will think the place is dirty.
7 My teacher was _____ when I got the highest mark. I'm usually near the bottom of the class.
8 My friends gave me a(n) _____ necklace for my birthday. It's so beautiful!
9 He discovered the origin of the legend when he read some _____ documents from the twelfth century.
10 The tube train gets so _____ in the rush hour that sometimes you can't even get on and have to wait for the next one.

VOCABULARY PLUS
TWO-PART PHRASES

7 A Match 1–10 with a)–j) to make two-part phrases.

1 again		**a)** tired
2 bright		**b)** bustle
3 hustle		**c)** square
4 loud		**d)** downs
5 fair	and	**e)** dine
6 round		**f)** again
7 sick		**g)** early
8 ups		**h)** round
9 give		**i)** clear
10 wine		**j)** take

B Complete the sentences with the phrases in Exercise 7A.

1 I've told you _____ not to leave your towel on the bathroom floor. Why do you still do it?
2 I really enjoy the _____ of the busy market on a Sunday morning.
3 The match was won _____ by the Italian team, according to the rules.
4 This connection is great – I can hear you _____.
5 The company will _____ the visiting delegates in the best restaurants.
6 We drove _____ the town but we couldn't find the hotel.
7 As a business, we've had our _____ but currently everything is going well.
8 There has to be some _____ if we want to reach an agreement.
9 We need to leave _____ before the morning traffic gets too heavy.
10 He's _____ of working nights and wants to change to a day job.

READING

1 Do the quiz.

HOW GOOD ARE YOU ... REALLY?

1 A man is running for a crowded train. You see him coming and you could stand in the door to stop it closing. You:

a) keep the door open for him with a smile.

b) leave the door but look apologetic when it shuts in his face.

c) turn away – if he hadn't been late, he wouldn't have this problem.

d) **deliberately** shut the door as the train's already running late and you need it to leave.

2 A colleague at work has **confided in you** that he's really struggling financially. It's his daughter's birthday in a week and he can't afford to buy her anything. You:

a) give him a loan out of your savings and offer to take him out for a coffee to **cheer him up**.

b) try to be sympathetic and make some suggestions for cheap gifts.

c) feel embarrassed and smile but change the conversation.

d) explain the dangers of debt to him – if he'd thought more about his spending, he wouldn't be in this position.

3 A wealthy woman, loaded with jewellery and expensive clothes, steps out of a taxi. As she leaves, a necklace drops to the floor. You:

a) **rush** after her and give her the necklace back with no thought of reward.

b) shout, 'Excuse me,' and worry what to do when she disappears from sight.

c) ignore the necklace – she clearly has too many things anyway – but decide you're not going to take it as you might be accused of stealing.

d) pick up the necklace, laugh at the woman's misfortune and say, 'She's got so much more money than me!'

4 A friend tells you that she's met this really fit man. You know the person in question, and that's he's not kind. You:

a) listen to her thoughts but firmly tell her not to **pursue** the relationship, even when she gets angry.

b) listen to her and suggest that he's not quite right but that ultimately, **it's up to her.**

c) sit and nod, and don't say a word about what you think. Who are you to judge anyway?

d) look at her impatiently. You're not really interested in her love life and you don't consider her a good friend anyway.

Results

Mostly a's: You may be going over the top with your good intentions, feeding people's bad habits and generally letting people take advantage of you.

Mostly b's: Your heart is in the right place, but you need to be careful that people don't take advantage of you.

Mostly c's: You tend to ignore other people's misfortune and distance yourself by not getting involved.

Mostly d's: You're mean! How can you treat people like that?!

2 Match the words in bold in the quiz with definitions 1–6.

1 continue with _____

2 go quickly _____

3 told you a secret
_____

4 it's her decision _____

5 intentionally _____

6 make him feel happier
_____

VOCABULARY

MONEY

3 Underline the correct alternatives to complete the sentences.

1 We can offer you a starting *salary/ income* of £25,000 the first year.

2 The *money/currency* of Thailand is the baht.

3 I spent nearly all my *savings/currency* on a new car.

4 He offered a *reward/donation* of £100 to the person who found his dog.

5 Entry is free but you are kindly asked to make a *salary/donation*.

6 If your annual *income/reward* is over £21,000, you have to pay twenty percent tax.

7 He was so poor he couldn't even *fund/afford* to buy new shoes.

8 Don't spend more than you earn or you'll always be in *debt/savings*.

4 Complete the article with the words in the box.

| wealth savings salaries reward |
| poverty fund donations debts |
| afford income |

Changing generations

Millennials, those born after 1980 and reaching adulthood at the turn of the century, have very different expectations to their parents. They often cannot
¹_____ to leave their parents' home, and many of those who do have their own homes live in ²_____ because the ³_____ they might earn are very low and often they have little hope of increasing their ⁴_____.
In many cases, the ⁵_____ for doing a good job is being allowed to stay in the company. Most of the young adults who have been to university have huge ⁶_____ to repay for their education and don't even dream of having ⁷_____ for the future. The government won't ⁸_____ projects for those who are nearly forty but these same people won't be able to retire at the same age as their parents do. However, they are very socially-aware and many of them make ⁹_____ to charity. They also travel more than previous generations and although they don't have financial ¹⁰_____, they have the compensation of enriching experiences that their parents never had.

GRAMMAR
THIRD AND MIXED CONDITIONALS

5 Match 1–5 with a)–j) to make sentences. Choose two possible endings for each sentence.

1 If the couple had talked about their problems,
2 If the students had paid more attention,
3 If they had taken the underground instead of the bus,
4 If the teachers hadn't been trained,
5 If the neighbours had listened to the flood warnings,

a) their classes wouldn't be so effective.
b) they wouldn't have been late for the meeting.
c) they would have found the difficult children hard to handle.
d) they wouldn't have got divorced.
e) they would have left their homes in time.
f) they'd still be together.
g) they would have realised that they had the test today.
h) their furniture would be safe.
i) they wouldn't feel unprepared.
j) they would be at work already.

6 Complete the third conditional sentences with the correct form of the verbs in brackets.

1 She _wouldn't have left_ (not leave) him alone in the house if she _had known_ (know) he was a thief.
2 If you _____ (not tell) him, he _____ (not be) angry.
3 If Tim _____ (feel) any sympathy for his friend, he _____ (help) him.
4 The tree _____ (not fall) if the wind _____ (not be) so strong.
5 If the fire _____ (start) on the ground floor, many people _____ (not escape).
6 We _____ (never/discover) the beautiful statues if we _____ (not visit) the old temple.
7 If she _____ (not stop) to talk to me, I _____ (not hear) the news about Larry.
8 If I _____ (not have) a compass, I _____ (lose) my way.
9 They _____ (not be) able to go on holiday if they _____ (not save) some money.
10 The plant _____ (not die) if you _____ (water) it more often.

WRITING
A THANK YOU MESSAGE; LEARN TO USE FORMAL/ INFORMAL EXPRESSIONS

7 Read the thank you messages below and answer the questions.
1 Which one is formal and which one is informal?
2 Which one is from a former employee to a boss?
3 Which one is from an exchange student to the family he stayed with?

A   To   Megan   From   Benji

Hi Megan,

Just writing to say thanks ever so much for everything last month. I had such a great time staying with you and getting to know your family. I can't wait to see you next month. We can party in a club and hang out with my friends.

Say hi to Steve from me!

Love,

Benji

B   To   Peter Sutton   From   Michael Gravy

Dear Mr Sutton,

I am writing to thank you **very** much for **providing** a reference for my job application. **I greatly appreciate your help. You will be pleased to hear that** I was offered the **position**.

Please do not hesitate to contact me if I can help you in return.

Yours sincerely,

Michael Gravy

8 A Imagine message B is from a former employee who has an informal relationship with his boss. Replace the phrases in bold with the phrases in the box.

ever so   giving   all the best   great news!   Hi Peter   Mike   just writing   job   your help is much appreciated   get in touch

B Rewrite message A to make it more formal. Use some of the phrases in the box.

warm regards   I'm looking forward to   go out in the evening   send my regards   thank you very much indeed   meeting   Dear   I am writing

9 Read the message and write a thank you message to Mrs Gordon.

Dear Ms Tully,
I attach a cheque for £500 as a contribution to your Children in Need fundraising project. I am afraid that I will not be able to participate as a volunteer, but I hope this donation will help you reach your target.
I look forward to receiving news of how the project is progressing.
Yours sincerely,
Emily Gordon (Mrs)

VOCABULARY

HAPPINESS

1 A Replace the words in bold in the sentences with the phrases with the opposite meaning in the box.

> takes great pleasure in   has a good time
> looks on the bright side of
> is contented with   is on top of the world
> lives in the moment

1 He's won the gold medal and **feels really depressed**. He's never been so happy.

2 He has such a positive attitude to life. He **finds something negative in** everything, even when it's been a disaster.

3 The shopkeeper **really hates** serving each customer personally.

4 She **doesn't enjoy herself** when she meets her friends at the weekend.

5 He always **worries about the future**, which helps him to make the most of every day.

6 She **feels dissatisfied with** what she has and doesn't expect anything more.

B Complete the conversations with the phrases in the box in Exercise 1A.

A: So, are you looking forward to the family reunion? Wow! Is your grandfather really going to be 100 years old?

B: Yes, he is! It's amazing, isn't it? And he ¹*takes great pleasure in* seeing us all, even though his hearing is not as good as it was. It should be fun to see my cousins again as well.

A: Oh yes, how's your cousin Ronnie? He went to live in Australia, didn't he?

B: Yeah, and he's really happy. In fact, he ² _____ because he's just got married.

A: That's great! What's his wife like?

B: She's the sort of person who always ³ _____ life, which balances Ronnie's negative personality.

A: So, it sounds like he ⁴ _____ his life abroad. And his sister, Jan?

B: Ah, Jan. You know she still ⁵ _____ and has few ambitions for the future. But she's coming especially from Scotland for the party.

A: Well, I hope your grandfather ⁶ _____ !

B: I'm sure he will.

FUNCTION

ASKING FOR AND EXPRESSING AGREEMENT/ DISAGREEMENT

2 Complete the questions with question tags.

1 This is a great party, _____ ?
2 You need to enjoy what you do, _____ ?
3 She didn't have fun, _____ ?
4 They're living in the countryside, _____ ?
5 He's got the best idea, _____ ?
6 Everything will be fine, _____ ?

3 A ▶ 6.2 Listen to six conversations. Do the speakers agree (A) or disagree (D)?

1 _____   3 _____   5 _____
2 _____   4 _____   6 _____

B Underline the correct alternatives to complete the conversations. Listen again and check your answers.

1 **A:** I reckon we should get out of the city next weekend.
  B: I *really/totally/very* agree. Let's go to the beach.

2 **A:** The best way to diet is to stop eating.
  B: I don't think *it/so/well*. You'll make yourself ill.

3 **A:** You need to accept your past and move on, don't you?
  B: *No way!/It really does!/Absolutely!* It's more important to look to the future.

4 **A:** Nothing's better than lying by a pool in the sun.
  B: That's *such a/so/much* true – and with a good book.

5 **A:** I think the government has made a mistake.
  B: I'd say the *opposite/truth/right*. They're doing a good job.

6 **A:** You should try salsa classes if you want to meet people.
  B: *No way!/That's right!/Totally!* I'm no good at dancing.

LEARN TO

AGREE USING SYNONYMS

4 A Match words 1–5 with their near synonyms a)–e).

1 salary   a) pleasure
2 ecological   b) natural
3 really cold   c) never on time
4 a good time   d) freezing
5 unpunctual   e) income

B Complete the conversations with the words in Exercise 4A.

1 **A:** It was _____ yesterday, wasn't it?
  B: Yeah, it was _____ . I had to wear ski socks!

2 **A:** He's late again! He's so _____ !
  B: I know. He's _____ .

3 **A:** The monthly _____ is very good in your new job, isn't it?
  B: Yes, I'll finally have a decent _____ .

4 **A:** You had _____ at the dinner, right?
  B: Yes, I did. It was a real _____ meeting everyone.

5 **A:** I think it's important to buy _____ produce.
  B: Absolutely! _____ products are much better for you.

VOCABULARY NATURE

1 Complete the sentences with the words in the box.

rainforest creature disease vegetation canopy parasite flood snake

1 Malaria is a terrible _____ which causes hundreds of thousands of deaths.
2 There is only one type of venomous _____ in the region and only one person has been bitten this year.
3 They couldn't see the sky through the thick _____ of trees above them.
4 The desert had little _____, so there was nowhere to shelter from the burning sun.
5 The flash _____ washed away the houses that had been built too close to the river.
6 Toxoplasmosis is an infection caused by a _____ that can be transmitted by cats.
7 For ecologists, the tropical _____ is one of the most important ecosystems in the world.
8 The jerboa is a strange _____. It looks like a mouse but jumps like a kangaroo.

GRAMMAR QUANTIFIERS

2 Circle the correct answer, a), b) or c), to complete the sentences.

1 There are _____ of mosquitoes in the region, so we had to sleep under nets.
   a) a large amount **b)** loads **c)** a great deal
2 Sadly, _____ people are aware of the poverty in the city centre.
   a) little **b)** few **c)** a few
3 Having _____ homework can make children stressed.
   a) too much **b)** too many **c)** enough
4 They saw _____ wildlife on the safari.
   a) a lot of **b)** much **c)** many
5 I tried calling you _____ times but you never answer your phone.
   a) much **b)** a great deal of **c)** several
6 The work experience gave him a _____ of confidence for job interviews.
   a) deal **b)** lot **c)** lots
7 We only got _____ business from the new office we opened last year.
   a) much **b)** a little **c)** a few
8 I visited _____ historic sites on my trip to Athens.
   a) several **b)** an amount of **c)** little
9 The explorers found _____ of caves with drawings on the walls.
   a) an amount **b)** a great deal **c)** a number
10 I'd like to give you _____ tips before you start.
   a) much **b)** a couple of **c)** few

VOCABULARY TYPES OF PEOPLE

3 Complete the sentences. Use one word from box A and one word from box B in each gap. One of the compound nouns needs to be written as one word.

A computer book couch film beach

B bum potato nerd worm buff

1 My father didn't want to become a _____ when he retired, so he took up several sports.
2 I went to the south coast on holiday just to chill out and be a _____ for a week or two.
3 Everyone said she was a _____ because she always sat reading in the break time.
4 The new employee in IT is a real _____. He goes home and sits programming all evening.
5 He became a _____ after working in a cinema, where he could see whatever he wanted for free.

GRAMMAR -ING FORM AND INFINITIVE

4 Underline the correct alternatives to complete the sentences.

1 Jo didn't fancy *to come/coming* to the concert.
2 He *looks forward/hopes* to meeting you next week.
3 I'm calling *telling/to tell* you the news.
4 They managed *to find/finding* their way home.
5 The little girl *refused/enjoyed* to speak to her teacher.
6 I've got a new job far away from home, so I miss not *to walk/walking* to work.
7 You mustn't give up *to try/trying* to pass your exam.
8 In winter they tend not *to go/going* to bed late.
9 She *imagined/decided* to be an airline pilot.
10 The journey seemed *to go on/going on* forever.

VOCABULARY PLUS FORMAL VS INFORMAL REGISTER

5 Underline the correct alternatives to complete the sentences.

1 They can easily afford a holiday in the Caribbean because they're *slobs/loaded*.
2 He's a real *try-hard/hassle* with the boss and always agrees with everything she says.
3 It's interesting to spend time with him because he's really *fit/chatty* and has lots to say.
4 I spent the weekend *vegging out/go-getting* at home, just watching TV and eating nice food.
5 I was still wearing my pyjamas when she came over at midday. I felt like such a *slob/go-getter*.
6 My idea of a good evening is listening to peaceful music and just *hassling/chilling*.

VOCABULARY SOCIETY

6 Complete the words in the sentences about important issues. The first letter of each word is given.

1 The main issue that worries young people is u_____ because there are very few jobs.

2 On one channel they said there were 2,000 demonstrators, on the other 10,000. I hate it when there is media m_____ of facts.

3 With the new hospital they have built in the town, our h_____ facilities have improved tremendously.

4 It's unfair that a few people in the country are very rich while the rest are living in p_____ with no money and barely enough to eat.

5 My computer went off because of a p_____ c_____, so I lost all my unsaved work.

6 Don't criticise the government in public here because you'll be arrested. There's no f_____ o___ s_____ in this country.

FUNCTION EXPRESSING YOUR OPINION

7 Correct the underlined mistakes in the conversations.

1 **A:** What shall we do <u>for</u> the traffic problem?
   B: As I <u>think</u> it, the first thing is to persuade people to use public transport.

2 **A:** Well, we must <u>to give</u> the children priority.
   B: That's a fair <u>ask</u>, but the whole family needs help.

3 **A:** I <u>seem</u> that the government is not dealing well with the issue.
   B: That <u>can</u> be true, but it is a complicated problem.

4 **A:** You can <u>know</u> it from me that the newspapers have manipulated the story.
   B: Well, if you <u>tell</u> me, the president should explain what is really happening.

GRAMMAR MODALS OF DEDUCTION

8 Match questions 1–6 with answers a)–f). Then underline the correct alternatives to complete the answers.

1 Why is Steve taking so long to reply?
2 What do you think Gail is doing now she's on holiday?
3 When do you think he'll get here?
4 How long does the journey to Barcelona take?
5 How does he manage to run marathons every month?
6 Who's knocking at the door?

a) I'm sure she *should/will* be sitting on a beach somewhere.

b) I suppose he *can/might* need to consult his boss before giving you an answer.

c) He *can/must* have a lot of energy.

d) He *couldn't/could* arrive at any moment.

e) That *won't/will* be Mary. She said she was coming this afternoon.

f) On a good day it should take about thirty minutes by car but if there's traffic, it *might/must* take longer.

VOCABULARY EXTREME ADJECTIVES

9 Underline the correct alternatives to complete the sentences.

1 The film was about a *packed/gigantic* meteorite that was on a path to destroy the Earth.

2 His kitchen is always *filthy/spotless*. I don't know how he manages to keep it so clean.

3 Every day there are appeals on the TV to help the *gigantic/starving* children in Africa.

4 If you wear those *filthy/spotless* jeans to the interview, you won't make a good impression.

5 I think spiders are *hideous/gorgeous* creatures with those horrible eyes and furry legs.

6 I was so *terrified/astonished* by the news of her marriage that I nearly fell off my chair.

7 She looked over the bridge and saw the *packed/terrifying* drop to the river below and thought she'd never be brave enough to jump.

8 You have to come shopping with me to buy the *hideous/gorgeous* red shoes I found in a shop on the High Street.

VOCABULARY PLUS TWO-PART PHRASES

10 The expressions in bold are in the wrong sentences. Correct them.

1 The best way to keep the delegates happy at the conference is to **give and take** them in a good restaurant in the evening.

2 I knocked on the door **round and round** until my hand hurt, but no one answered.

3 She's given her opinion **fair and square**. There's no doubt about how she feels.

4 We leave **ups and downs**, so remember to pack your case the night before.

5 He watched the **sick and tired** in the street and wondered where everyone was going.

6 The manager is **bright and early** of his staff chatting when they should be working.

7 You've beaten me **again and again**. It was a good match!

8 I walked **loud and clear** the building but all the doors were locked.

9 We've had our **hustle and bustle**, but at the moment our relationship is good.

10 We can come to an agreement with a bit of **wine and dine**. We all have to compromise.

VOCABULARY MONEY

11 Complete the sentences with the words in the box.

> savings afford reward donation fund wealth
> income poverty currency salary

1 Engineering students expect to find a job with a good _____ after the finish their studies.
2 He decided to give up one of his three jobs even though it meant a drop in _____.
3 Although there is no financial _____ for volunteering, it can be very satisfying.
4 We need a loan of £10,000 to _____ the purchase of new machinery.
5 A man came to my house yesterday asking for a(n) _____ for the Red Cross.
6 She couldn't _____ to buy a house, so she had to rent a place.
7 I was shocked by the obvious _____ in the city. There were lots of people sleeping on the streets.
8 Every month he put a few pounds in a(n) _____ account for his children's education.
9 I'd never heard of the naira, the _____ of Nigeria.
10 He was accused of tax evasion when they found most of his _____ in bank accounts abroad.

GRAMMAR THIRD AND MIXED CONDITIONALS

12 Rewrite the sentences using the third conditional or a mixed conditional.

1 She's in prison because she stole the car.
  If she *hadn't* stolen the car, she *wouldn't be* in prison.
2 He didn't get the job because he didn't wear a tie.
  If he _____ a tie, he _____ the job.
3 He has a beautiful house because he married a millionaire.
  He _____ a beautiful house if he _____ a millionaire.
4 They're stuck in traffic because they didn't leave before the rush hour.
  If they _____ before the rush hour, they _____ stuck in traffic.
5 The company lost a good customer because he forgot to phone her.
  They company _____ a good customer if he _____ to phone her.
6 I became famous because I was in the right place at the right time.
  If I _____ in the right place at the right time, I _____ famous.
7 We aren't in London because we missed our flight.
  We _____ in London if we _____ our flight.
8 You aren't studying abroad because you didn't apply for an Erasmus scholarship.
  If you _____ for an Erasmus scholarship, you _____ studying abroad.

VOCABULARY HAPPINESS

13 Match sentences 1–5 with paragraphs a)–e).
1 They're having a good time.
2 They're living in the moment.
3 They're on top of the world.
4 They look on the bright side of life.
5 They take great pleasure in something in their lives.

a) They seem to be very chilled, not really worried that they might not have enough money next year. They just enjoy travelling from place to place and picking up a job when they can.
b) They have finally finished and the graduation ceremony was so emotional. I can imagine that feeling of relief and satisfaction as they all throw their hats in the air and celebrate. It's a special moment.
c) They find it so relaxing just working in the garden at weekends, planting and watering the beautiful flowers. What they really love is the vegetable patch where they have all the produce they need.
d) The trip has been a great success so far. We took the children rafting yesterday and today they are going to the amusement park. It's been a great end-of-year holiday.
e) Despite having constant medical issues, they're so positive about the future. They say they're happy because if they hadn't been in hospital on the same day, they would never have met each other and that's what makes them lucky in life.

FUNCTION ASKING FOR AND EXPRESSING AGREEMENT/DISAGREEMENT

14 Underline the correct alternatives to complete the conversations.
1 A: This is a great film *is/isn't* it?
  B: Yes, it's *fantastic/awful*.
2 A: I *reckon/tell* the motorway will be the quickest way to get there.
  B: I don't think *so/that*. The traffic is terrible at this time of day.
3 A: He's going to offer a reward, *hasn't/isn't* he?
  B: *Absolutely/No way*! He's got no money.
4 A: Emily wasn't happy we forgot her birthday, *didn't/was* she?
  B: *Tell/Say* me about it! She hasn't spoken to me all day.

CHECK

Circle the correct answer, a), b) or c), to complete the sentences.

1 The heavy rain caused the worst ___ of the decade.
   a) canopy   b) floods   c) disease

2 I was only given a ___ of information just before the interview.
   a) little   b) few   c) bit

3 He really didn't know ___ about the situation.
   a) a lot of   b) many   c) much

4 The ticket inspector discovered that ___ of the passengers hadn't paid.
   a) couple   b) several   c) amount

5 The historical background to the novel was ___ so I learnt a lot.
   a) well-researched   b) slow-moving
   c) unconvincing

6 I thought he was a complete ___ but then I found he had many interests apart from computers.
   a) couch potato   b) nerd   c) buff

7 My mother tends ___ anxious if I don't phone her once a week.
   a) getting   b) to get   c) get

8 She opened the door quietly so as ___ the baby.
   a) for not waking   b) for not wake   c) not to wake

9 I can't ___ to go away with you for a month!
   a) imagine   b) agree   c) stand

10 She must be ___ . Just look at her designer clothes!
   a) loaded   b) chatty   c) fit

11 The previous manager was a ___ , so I hope the new one works harder and looks smarter.
   a) try-hard   b) go-getter   c) slob

12 There is a serious ___ problem in the area for the urban planning department.
   a) unemployment   b) poverty   c) housing

13 If you ___ me, there should be more police on the streets.
   a) ask   b) demand   c) tell

14 I think Ken ___ have the answer to your question.
   a) shan't   b) may   c) can

15 I'm sure they ___ be happy to hear they didn't win.
   a) won't   b) mustn't   c) might

16 They ___ train hard because they win every match.
   a) must   b) should   c) can

17 The train was absolutely ___, with rubbish on the floor and dirty windows.
   a) packed   b) hideous   c) filthy

18 She was ___ because she hadn't expected to see him.
   a) starving   b) astonished   c) awful

19 He's ___ of the two-hour journey to work every day.
   a) fair and square   b) sick and tired
   c) bright and early

20 Her annual ___ includes a share of the profits from the business.
   a) reward   b) debt   c) income

21 I had to use some of my ___ to pay for the repairs to my car.
   a) currency   b) wealth   c) savings

22 If he'd read the instructions, he ___ the machine.
   a) wouldn't have broken
   b) wouldn't break   c) hadn't broken

23 If Jan hadn't forgotten her passport, she ___ sitting crying in the airport now.
   a) wouldn't have been
   b) wouldn't be   c) would be

24 I ___ him a lift if my sister hadn't taken my car.
   a) had given   b) would have given
   c) wouldn't give

25 I really ___ everything you've done for us.
   a) appreciate   b) grateful   c) regards

26 It's better to look on the ___ side of things rather than focus on the bad.
   a) pleasant   b) bright   c) best

27 It's been good working from home for a few days,
   a) isn't it   b) wasn't it   c) hasn't it

28 The best players come from Italy, ___?
   a) do they   b) don't they   c) are they

29 I totally ___ with Ann about the danger of swimming in that river.
   a) reckon   b) agree   c) convince

30 'Let's try kite-surfing.' '___! I'd be terrified.'
   a) No way   b) Not necessarily
   c) I doubt it

RESULT   /30

7 ARTS

GRAMMAR

MAKING COMPARISONS; SO/SUCH

1 Underline the correct alternatives to complete the sentences.

1 This is the *less/least* expensive watch in the collection.
2 The installation was as big *than/as* an apartment.
3 His style was more modern *than/that* the other artists' creations.
4 I found the photos of war scenes *so/such* moving I nearly cried.
5 There were *more/many* oil paintings in the collection than sketches.
6 Each self-portrait was *more big/bigger* than the previous one.
7 The artist used *such/so* many beautiful colours in the collage.
8 I think her paintings are even *as/more* original than Dali's work.
9 He worked so *hard/harder* that he made himself ill.
10 I saw *such a/a so* wonderful exhibition last week.

2 Join the sentences using *so* or *such*. More than one answer may be possible.

1 The film was boring. I fell asleep.

_____
_____

2 He had a good time in Paris. He wants to go back there again.

_____
_____

3 The river is wide. We can't cross it.

_____
_____

4 There were a lot of problems with the design. They couldn't make it work.

_____
_____

5 She spoke fast. I didn't understand her.

_____
_____

6 The weather was terrible. We couldn't go for a walk.

_____
_____

7 My father's got a calm manner. He never gets angry.

_____
_____

3 Complete the sentences. Use the correct form of the adjectives in the box and one or two other words.

| long slow big comfortable exhausting brave complicated detailed fast loud |

1 The situation was _____ that we didn't know what to do.
2 The journey didn't take _____ as we expected.
3 The map was _____ that you could see every tiny street.
4 There was _____ noise that we all jumped in shock.
5 This is _____ computer on the market that only takes microseconds to process information.
6 He wanted a(n) _____ chair because his old one was giving him back problems.
7 Is this train always _____? I thought we'd be there by now.
8 It was _____ day that I fell asleep on the sofa when I got home.
9 The giant had eyes _____ as plates.
10 The soldier was given a medal for being _____ officer in his company.

LISTENING

4 A ▶ 7.1 Listen to a conversation between four friends about art galleries they have visited. Match speakers 1–4 with galleries a)–d).

1 Nick _____ 2 Jenny _____ 3 Max _____ 4 Sally _____

a) The Barcelona Museum of Contemporary Art
b) The Art Gallery of new South Wales in Sydney
c) The National Portrait Gallery in London
d) The Guggenheim Museum in New York

B Listen again and underline the correct alternatives.

1 Nick went to an exhibition of Cezanne's *portraits/sketches*.
2 Nick said it was hard to see the paintings well because of the *crowds/light*.
3 The exhibition *Under the Surface* that Jenny saw included a blue *sculpture/installation*.
4 Some of the art made Jenny feel *emotional/motivated*.
5 The exhibit Max saw of a cage represented *survival/cruelty*.
6 Max *didn't enjoy/absolutely loved* the exhibition.
7 Sally saw a special exhibition of *Australian art/self-portraits*.
8 Sally thinks fifteenth century art is *always/sometimes* interesting.

5 Read extracts 1–6 from the recording. Match the words/phrases in bold with definitions a)–f).

1 He used really thick **strokes**.
2 People just kept getting **in the way**.
3 I can't **pretend** to understand modern art.
4 It made such an **impact** on me.
5 It wasn't **my cup of tea**.
6 It's like she's **staring** straight at me.

a) in a position that stopped others from seeing
b) impression
c) claim
d) looking in a fixed way
e) movements of a brush when painting
f) something I like

VOCABULARY

VISUAL ARTS

6 Match the words in the box with photos A–H.

> self-portrait   canvas   paintbrush   installation
> charcoal   oil painting   sculpture   watercolour
> easel   sketch

A

B

1 _____
2 _____
3 _____
4 _____

C

D

5 _____
6 _____

E

F

7 _____
8 _____

G

H

9 _____
10 _____

7 Underline the correct alternatives to complete the sentences.

1 The famous modern painting consisted of a huge *canvas/easel* with a blue circle in the middle.
2 Andy Warhol produced many *self-portraits/multimedia* showing himself staring at the camera.
3 She used *watercolours/charcoal* to sketch her initial ideas for the painting.
4 Visitors could walk through the *oil painting/installation* that was set up in the entrance hall.
5 The children have worked hard to produce a *collage/canvas* from old newspapers and bottle tops.
6 She specialises in *multimedia/self-portrait* art, using recycled materials and sound and lighting effects.
7 My *paintbrush/sculpture* was too hard, so I couldn't use it.
8 We need at least ten *watercolours/easels* for the art class if we have ten students.
9 They removed the thick paint from the *sketch/oil painting* and discovered a Rembrandt underneath.
10 Roman *canvases/sculptures* often depicted gods and goddesses.

VOCABULARY PLUS

MULTI-WORD VERBS 2

8 Circle the correct answer, a), b) or c), to complete the sentences.

1 He came _____ a great idea for the company logo.
   a) out of   b) up with   c) along to
2 If you want to find an inexpensive phone, you'll have to shop _____, both online and in the stores.
   a) around   b) over   c) on
3 She has to look _____ her little sister because her parents work long hours.
   a) for   b) after   c) into
4 I couldn't play in the tennis match and I felt terrible about _____ my tennis partner down.
   a) letting   b) giving   c) doing
5 It was a good offer. Why did you turn it _____?
   a) over   b) up   c) down
6 I pressed the button five times but the TV still didn't turn _____, so I couldn't watch anything.
   a) in   b) on   c) off
7 We'd planned a barbecue in the garden but we had to _____ off the party because it was raining.
   a) turn   b) call   c) send
8 She thought she could count _____ him but he didn't help at all in the end.
   a) with   b) _____ in   c) _____ on
9 Don't throw _____ those old clothes. I'm sure we can donate them to a charity.
   a) away   b) around   c) about
10 He didn't want to say where he had been, so he made _____ a story about having to go to hospital.
   a) over   b) in   c) up

VOCABULARY

MUSIC

1 A Put the letters in brackets in the correct order to complete the text.

Music update

So, now for the highlights of this month's music scene. First up we have a new ¹_____ (karct) from Mickey. Following his move into ²_____ (nehtco) music, this one will certainly be played in any ³_____ (vera) party you go to this summer. You can ⁴_____ (addnowol) it free on our website.

For those who prefer ⁵_____ (par), check out the ⁶_____ (malub) from KZ, which has ⁷_____ (cylisr) about the current political situation. It's on its way to ⁸_____ (ebnurm) one already!

Last but not least, ⁹_____ (nasf) of Telling Tales will enjoy their latest ¹⁰_____ (endac) music recordings. Turn the ¹¹_____ (keaprsse) up to full volume and the ¹²_____ (yhhtrm) will certainly get everyone moving in the clubs!

B Complete the sentences with words from Exercise 1A.

1 I tried to _____ the music from iTunes but my internet connection was too slow.

2 There is one _____ on the CD that I love – the others aren't very good.

3 That song has been _____ one for three weeks already.

4 My favourite _____ is his second one, which includes those great love songs.

5 The drummer kept the _____ going well but the guitarist kept missing the beat.

6 I don't mind listening to foreign music; even if I don't understand the _____, I can appreciate the sound.

7 There were hundreds of _____ sleeping on the street the night before the concert.

8 The music system has excellent _____ that produce great quality sound.

9 They rented an old warehouse for the _____ party and 1,000 people spent the night dancing there.

10 A lot of _____ lyrics are written to give voice to a social message.

11 I think _____ music is too repetitive and I don't like the electronic sound much.

12 All the best _____ music DJs, such as Calvin Harris and David Guetta, like playing in Ibiza in the summer.

READING

Glastonbury Festival

Tents, terrible toilets, great bands, singing the lyrics to your favourite tracks, mud and more mud! That's what most people associate with the famous Glastonbury festival, which takes place every summer at Worthy Farm near Glastonbury in the west of England.

The early years . . . .

The festival is probably the best-known music festival in the UK. It used to attract hippies in the 1970s and the first show was held the day after Jimi Hendrix died in 1970. This first festival was called The Pilton Pop, Blues & Folk Festival and tickets cost £1. There were four festivals held in the seventies, including one unplanned event in 1971, where 500 people **turned up** at the farm and set up a stage.

The eighties – the festival grows . . . .

By 1982 tickets cost £8 and numbers were steadily growing as fans **flocked** from all over the country to see some of their favourite artists playing live. In these early years the number of **gatecrashers** was almost the same as the number of ticket holders as people jumped over the fences into the farm without paying. In 1981 a local farmer, Michael Eavis, who owns the site, took control of the event. In 1985 the festival grew too large for Worthy Farm and so the next-door farm was bought as well. That year it rained hard and as the mud mixed with the cow dung from the dairy farm, it made a smelly mixture: festival-goers had to get used to being filthy and squelching as they walked to their tents.

The nineties – changing styles . . . .

The rain didn't stop people coming back and by the early nineties unofficial sound systems began to pop up with people playing acid house music through powerful speakers. Some found this sort of music threatening, but once the festival was widely televised in 1994, the initial folk and rock music flavour of the festival disappeared as more **mainstream** dance music bands became the main attractions. People could now see what a rave looked like and be part of the experience. 1997 was the year of major mud, but it is still remembered as a great festival, with Radiohead **headlining** on the famous Pyramid Stage – said to be one of the greatest ever performances at Glastonbury.

The twenty-first century – a modern event . . . .

In 2000 250,000 fans attended the festival but only 100,000 tickets were actually sold, so the organisers realised they had to do something about the gatecrashers. They built a high security fence around the festival site and attendance has remained at around 135,000 people since then. Over the years it has become harder and harder to get tickets and in 2017 100,000 tickets were sold online in under an hour. Some bands record special Glastonbury albums and the groups range widely from techno played at the Silver Hayes area to grime and hip hop artists such as Stormzy performing on the main stages. There is something for everyone and the event raises millions for charities. It has come a long way from its hippy **roots** – now you can even download an app to work out what you want to see.

2 Read the article and answer the questions.

1 What kind of music was played at the early festival?_____

2 Why did the farmer, Michael Eavis, buy the land next to Worthy Farm? _____

3 What kind of music was played unofficially at the beginning of the nineties? _____

4 How could people watch the festival without actually attending in the mid-nineties?

_____

5 How many people paid to attend the festival in 2000? _____

6 How long did it take to sell most of the tickets in 2017? _____

7 How can you find out who's playing at the festival nowadays? _____

3 Underline the correct alternatives to complete the definitions of the words/phrases in bold in the article.

1 turned up: appeared *unexpectedly/quickly*

2 flocked: came *very quickly/in large numbers*

3 gatecrashers: people who enter an event *without a ticket/through the wrong entrance*

4 mainstream: *alternative/currently popular*

5 headlining: being the *most important/loudest* band in a festival

6 roots: *disasters/origins*

GRAMMAR

BE/GET USED TO VS USED TO

4 Complete the sentences with the correct form of *be/get used to* or *used to* and the verbs in brackets.

1 It took me a few weeks but I eventually _____ (sleep) on a futon when I lived in Japan.

2 When I was a child, I _____ (eat) lots of sweet things, so now my teeth aren't good.

3 She never _____ (drink) tea but now she lives in India and drinks it a lot.

4 She moved from the city to a small village. It was difficult at first but now she _____ (live) there.

5 In Britain we drive on the left, so when I came to France, I had to _____ (drive) on the right.

6 When I first started work as a doctor, I _____ (work) nights but nowadays I only have a day shift.

7 As a soldier, you have to _____ (take) orders.

8 I found it difficult to walk in my new shoes because I _____ (not wear) high heels.

9 We _____ (enjoy) going to Wales on holiday when I was a child.

10 It was hard when my children left home but I slowly _____ (live) alone.

WRITING

AN ESSAY; LEARN TO USE PARALLELISM

5 Read the essay and put the paragraphs in the correct order (1–5).

Should music and art be taught at secondary school?

A Although there are clearly wider-reaching benefits for both subjects, some people argue that secondary school is so demanding in other areas that students cannot afford the time for more artistic subjects if they have no intention of following a career in those fields. However, if they don't have encouragement to develop all aspects of their creative ability in the school environment, then they are unlikely to start when they are older. We know that a scientist needs [1]**a knowledge of history and a knowledge of language** to be able to understand concepts and express them, so why don't they need a creative stimulus too?

B How useful is it to study music and art at school? The fact is that very few secondary school students study music and art nowadays. I feel that this is a negative development as there are many reasons why it is important to develop students' interest in these subjects at this age.

C Firstly, we need to examine the benefits of music that go far beyond the simple enjoyment of the subject. [2]**The rhythm of music and the rhythm of language** have a lot in common and music helps the part of the brain that processes language develop more effectively. Not only that, but mathematics is used to create music [3]**with patterns, with intervals and with structure**. If you can become good at understanding those patterns, you are going to be good at understanding them in other situations.

D In conclusion, while it may be thought that these subjects [4]**should be studied after school or they can be learnt at weekends**, just like training for a sport or hiking with the Scouts, I am convinced that schools should find the time and resources to give their students an education that is as complete as possible, and this means including both music and art in the curriculum.

E Secondly, it should be recognised that art can also help with other subjects. Art is so much more than learning to draw and paint. It encourages concentration and develops students' capacity for expression [5]**and you can become more creative**. It can help you see the world in a new way and can encourage ideas and concepts to come alive, which can then be transferred to science or the study of literature.

6 Rewrite the phrases in bold in the essay using parallelism. Be careful with phrase 5 – you need to change an adjective to a noun.

1 *a knowledge of history and a knowledge of language =*
a knowledge of history and language

7 Write an essay (200–250 words) on this question.

Should museums and art galleries be free for everyone?

VOCABULARY
EVERYDAY OBJECTS

1 Complete the sentences. Use one word from box A and one word from box B in each gap.

A
clothes   rubbish   electric   tea   hair   watering paper   wrapping   price

B
bag   paper   bin   peg   can   tag   dryer towel   fan

1 To make a perfect afternoon drink, you only need one _____ in a cup of hot water.

2 I was annoyed when there was no _____ in my hotel room, so I had to go out looking awful.

3 Have you got any _____ for the present I bought for Tom?

4 Can you pass me one more _____ to hang out this shirt?

5 I don't like air-conditioning but I do have a powerful _____ for when it's hot.

6 I was embarrassed when I realised I had left the _____ on the back of my new dress.

7 My aunt loves gardening, so I gave her a(n) _____ for Christmas.

8 She used a(n) _____ to clean up the water on the floor because she didn't have a sponge.

9 I threw Joe's socks into the _____ by mistake.

FUNCTION
RESPONDING TO SUGGESTIONS

2 A ▶ 7.2 Listen to three friends planning an event at an art college. Match places 1–6 with the things that will go there a)–f).

Alton Art College – End of term show

Saturday 15th June
10a.m.–5p.m.
All welcome!

1	Room 1	**a)**	installation
2	Room 2	**b)**	tables and chairs
3	Room 3	**c)**	water colour exhibition
4	Room 4	**d)**	children's workshop
5	Room 5	**e)**	oil painting demonstration
6	outside	**f)**	multimedia exhibition

B How did the speakers respond to suggestions? Complete the responses. Listen again and check your answers.

1 A: Won't it fit in Room 5? It's quite big and we need the hall space free.
   B: That's a g_____ i_____.

2 A: They could go outside, round the back.
   B: That sounds s_____.

3 A: I'd say Room 2 is best. The sun is on that side in the morning.
   B: E_____!

4 A: We can use Room 3 for the children's workshop, can't we?
   B: I'm not so s_____.

5 A: We can set up the easel there.
   B: That s_____ perfect.

6 A: The projector broke down last week and it's still being repaired.
   B: Are you s_____?

7 A: We'll have to call off the multimedia event.
   B: How a_____!

8 A: I'm sure they'll lend us one.
   B: That's s_____ a good idea, Charlie!

LEARN TO
AGREE USING ME TOO/ME NEITHER

3 Complete the conversations with *do, don't, too* or *neither*.

1 A: I want to go out for a walk.
   B: I _____. It's raining!

2 A: I adore this sculpture.
   B: Me _____. It's amazing!

3 A: I don't like doing these experiments.
   B: I _____. It's fascinating!

4 A: I just love walking in the rain!
   B: Me _____. This is fun!

5 A: I can't stand biology. It's so boring!
   B: Me _____. I just don't understand anything.

6 A: I think modern art is exciting.
   B: I _____. I mean, a child could make something better than that.

LISTENING

 1 A Look at some of the animals from Aesop's fables (stories by an ancient Greek storyteller). Match animals 1–6 with pictures A–F.

1 grasshopper _____   4 stork _____
2 fox _____   5 hare _____
3 ant _____   6 tortoise _____

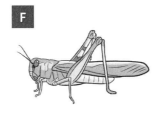

B ▶ 8.1 Listen to two people talking about Aesop's fables. Write the animal pairs next to morals 1–3. Then answer question 4.

1 Treat others like you want them to treat you.

_____

2 Slow and steady wins the race.

_____

3 It's best to prepare for times of necessity.

_____

4 Which natural forces are used to demonstrate the saying 'Persuasion is better than force'?

_____

C Listen again and complete the sentences.

1 The ant spent all summer _____ food.
2 The grasshopper _____ all summer.
3 In the winter the grasshopper _____.
4 The hare _____ in the middle of the race.
5 The story of the hare and the tortoise helped Judy with _____.
6 No one wanted to work with Sarah because she had _____.
7 The class learnt to be _____ from the story of the fox and the stork.
8 In the story of the sun and the wind, the man took his coat off because he was _____.

VOCABULARY

LEXICAL CHUNKS WITH MAKE, DO, TAKE

2 Complete the sentences with *make*, *do* or *take*.

1 The fire will _____ terrible damage to the ecosystem in the area if we can't get it under control.
2 The political parties will have to _____ pact because none of them has a majority in the parliament.
3 His mother thought he could _____ nothing wrong until she realised he'd been stealing.
4 You'll have to train really hard and _____ your utmost to win.
5 You shouldn't _____ it for granted that New Year's Day will be a holiday because we might ask you to work.
6 The people in the town won't _____ the warning seriously unless the police confirm the danger.
7 We've had to _____ some alterations to the schedule for next week to fit in an extra meeting.
8 The two businessmen knew they had to _____ a deal to protect both companies.
9 Passengers may _____ advantage of the VIP lounge before they fly.
10 Some people's aim in life is to _____ as much money as possible.

3 Complete the article with the phrases in the box.

> making an enormous amount of money
> make a deal   take the threat seriously
> have taken control of   took advantage of
> have done their utmost   did nothing wrong
> have done tremendous damage

No end to the war

Latest reports from the north of the region is that the rebels [1]_____ the oilfields and [2]_____ to the infrastructures in the city. People have criticised the army because they didn't [3]_____ enough and although they [4]_____ to recapture the city, the rebels clearly [5]_____ their lack of organisation. However, the government claims that the army generals [6]_____ and are prepared to [7]_____ with the rebels to try and achieve peace. Meanwhile, it is clear that arms manufacturers are [8]_____ from the situation.

GRAMMAR
RELATIVE CLAUSES

4 Underline the correct alternatives to complete the sentences .
1 The bus, *which/that* was full, took three hours to get there.
2 I'd like the dress *that/when* you showed me earlier.
3 My brother Nick, *who/that* lives in Australia, is a doctor.
4 This book is the one *what/that* I was telling you about.
5 That is the manager *whose/who's* work produced great results last year.
6 I feel like going to some place *which/where* I can rest.

5 Complete the sentences with relative pronouns.
1 The rebels, _____ had hidden in the forest, appeared that night.
2 I'd like to speak to the person _____ is responsible for staff.
3 Where is the patient _____ bed is empty?
4 The city _____ I live is enormous.
5 1986 was the year _____ the president was assassinated.
6 The farm house, _____ was abandoned, stood at the top of a hill.

6 Join the sentences using relative clauses. Use the second sentence in each pair for the relative clause.
1 I want to meet the man. You were talking to him yesterday.
 I want to meet the man who you were talking to yesterday.
2 My brother got married last year. His wife is from Mexico.
_____
3 That's the village. My grandparents used to live there.
_____
4 The painting was sold for a million pounds. It had been hidden for years.
_____
5 That was the moment. I realised he was leaving.
_____
6 Jeff has bought a new computer. You met him yesterday.
_____
7 Have you seen the girl? Her bag is on the table.
_____
8 They phoned the company. It offered cheap flights.
_____

WRITING
ANECDOTE; LEARN TO SET THE SCENE

7 A ▶ 8.2 Read the anecdote. Then listen to the end of the story and choose the best title, a), b), c) or d).
a) Ghosts from the past c) A lucky escape
b) Travelling in time d) A lesson learnt

This must have been **about five years ago** when I was working in Paris for a multi-national. It was a cool summer morning as I set off to get the train for the airport to go to a business meeting in London. I got to the station in plenty of time and **was just about to** go through the ticket barrier when I realised I'd left my tickets in my desk in my office. So, I turned around and rushed back. Luckily, the office wasn't far away, so I could walk there.

As I was hurrying down the street, I was stopped by a woman who said, 'Excuse me. Haven't we met before?' I had no idea who she was but she had clear blue eyes and looked at me with a surprising intensity. **At first,** I apologised saying, 'I'm sorry, I don't think so,' but she continued to stare at me and then said, 'I think you should take your time to get to your meeting today.' Confused, I said, 'Why would I do that?' She answered, 'The voices are telling me.'

At the time, I thought she must be a bit crazy, ignored her and continued walking back to the office, but I felt a bit strange, so I went slowly, thinking that maybe she was familiar after all.

Anyway, I got in to work, picked up my papers from my desk and started back to the station. **It was then that** I heard the sirens and saw the ambulances and police cars passing me down the road …

B Read the anecdote again and put the sentences in order (1–7).
a) He went to the station for the first time.
b) He met a woman.
c) He was going to his office.
d) He left his tickets in the office. *1*
e) He had a strange feeling.
f) He looked for the woman.
g) There was an explosion.

C Match the time phrases in bold in the anecdote with phrases 1–6 that could replace them.
1 initially 4 that was when
2 around 2013 5 was going to
3 at that moment 6 while

D Answer the questions about the anecdote.
1 Where did the story take place?
2 What was the writer doing there?
3 Who were the people in the story?
4 What do we know about the appearance of the woman?
5 What impression did the writer have of the woman?

8 Write an anecdote about a trip you made when something pleasant or unpleasant happened (250–300 words). Remember to set the scene with information about the time, the sequence of events, the place and the people.

READING

1 A Read the article. Choose the best sentence, a), b) or c), to summarise the writer's idea.

a) The way you say something can alter the meaning.

b) Images are more powerful than words.

c) Don't always trust what you read or hear.

B Complete the sentences with the words in the box.

> emotional   be lost   a lot of   don't always

1 It is unlikely that many pets will _____ in the coming year.

2 We often use _____ words to convince others.

3 To get a good idea of public opinion, _____ people should be asked.

4 Journalists _____ report the news they find out about.

C Match the words/phrases in bold in the article with definitions 1–5.

1 a study of people's opinions   _____

2 support your way of thinking   _____

3 interesting as news   _____

4 giving the wrong impression   _____

5 result   _____

GRAMMAR

FUTURE FORMS

2 Circle the correct answer, a), b) or c), to complete the sentences.

1 The teacher _____ be furious when he hears the news about the school closing.
a) will may   **b)** is due to
c) will probably

2 Do you think she _____ go out with me if I ask her?
a) might   **b)** is bound to   **c)** going to

3 According to the timetable, the plane is _____ arrive at 8p.m. tonight.
a) due to   **b)** bound to   **c)** about to

4 He was _____ to explain the problem when she interrupted him and didn't let him speak.
a) likely   **b)** about   **c)** maybe

5 Scientists predict that the sea level _____ rise in the next few decades.
a) is about to   **b)** is due to   **c)** will

6 There's a train strike, so the meeting _____ start late today.
a) is likely to   **b)** probably won't
c) is about to

The power of words (and numbers)

'Twenty percent of the population will lose their beloved pet in the next year.' Now we're worried. It sounds like very soon our little dog may no longer be with us. But wait a minute – does it mean we're going to lose our dog, someone is bound to steal our dog, our dog is going to die or we're about to give away our dog because we're moving away or too elderly to take care of it?

Words are powerful, but they can also be **misleading**. Never more so than in politics where figures are manipulated to serve the interests of

Government statistics show that the less time people spend travelling by car, the fewer accidents they will have.

Should I drive faster?

a political party. When you survey a number of people, there are lots of ways of making the results **fit your agenda**, or report the situation using the words you want people to hear. If a politician wanted to increase spending on the police force, he or she might say, 'Hundreds of people are terrified to leave their homes at night,' while omitting to tell us that hundreds more feel quite safe.

These statements play on emotions rather than being based on facts. Even if they are based on facts, they are often not based on all of the facts. Then there are the people who are asked questions in a **poll** or survey. If only fifty people are asked, they will not represent the opinion of everyone. For an accurate poll to be carried out, enough people need to be asked, but also a variety of people: it might be that the poll is carried out during the day when a lot of people are at work, so the answers only represent those who do not work.

Newspapers need to have sensational stories to sell papers, so

The latest survey indicates that the people who have the most birthdays live the longest.

YEARS OF LIFE

NO. OF BIRTHDAYS

if the statistics aren't **newsworthy**, they won't publish them. This means that sometimes new statistics are ignored. On other occasions, politicians will deliberately ignore results of polls if they don't support their argument, or polls can be re-done with different questions to get a different **outcome**.

It's all about how you look at it. If your son comes home and says, 'I got sixty-seven percent, which is a B,' you are likely to be pleased – until you find out that every other member of the class got an A.

VOCABULARY

CRITICAL THINKING

3 Complete the sentences with the words in the box.

rational   accurate   misleading   biased
reasonable   flawed   open-minded
reliable   well-informed   plausible

1 His opinion is _____ because he'll always support the left-wing party without question.

2 'I left my homework on the bus' is not a(n) _____ excuse. You always come by car.

3 She's very _____ and is never late.

4 His arguments are totally _____ because he has followed a logical process.

5 Do you think he's _____ enough to accept the cultural differences in his new post abroad?

6 He's _____ about the latest research and can tell you all you want to know.

7 The design of the machine was _____, so they had to return them all to the factory.

8 Without _____ sales figures we can't calculate our profit.

9 It's not _____ to ask employees to work twelve-hour days.

10 Statistics can often be _____ as they can be manipulated to give a false impression.

4 Underline the correct alternatives to complete the conversation between three detectives talking about a case.

Ann: So, how are you getting on with the investigation?

Rob: I've had some information from a source about the movements of one of the suspects, from his girlfriend.

Joe: Do you think she's ¹*reliable/accurate*? After all, she is his girlfriend, so she might tell us something ²*misleading/open-minded*.

Rob: You may be right. Perhaps the street cameras will give a more ³*accurate/well-informed* picture of where he was that night.

Joe: OK, I'll check. Now, I think the way the robbery was planned doesn't fit in with the way the mafia usually operates, so the theory about mafia involvement may be ⁴*rational/flawed*.

Ann: What do you mean?

Joe: Well, it's just not ⁵*plausible/reliable* that they would wear clown masks and escape on bicycles.

Ann: If you say so, but don't be ⁶*biased/reasonable*. We have to investigate all the possibilities.

Joe: Right, I'll be ⁷*accurate/open-minded* about that one. Now, the second suspect is a problem. He appears to be ⁸*well-informed/biased* about our plans, so every time we get close to him, he has already moved on.

Rob: The ⁹*rational/accurate* explanation for that one is that he has friends in the police force.

Ann: That's certainly a ¹⁰*reasonable/flawed* observation.

Joe: It is. Right, I'll look into it.

VOCABULARY PLUS

NUMBERS AND STATISTICS

5 A ▶ 8.3 Listen and complete the sentences with the numbers and units you hear.

1 Redwood trees can measure over _____ in height

2 The city of Jericho is over _____ old

3 The temperature on the surface of the sun is estimated to be nearly _____ Celsius,

4 Rainforests cover less than _____ of the world's land surface

5 To get into space, rockets must travel at _____ per second

6 A hurricane can be as large as _____ wide

7 Dinosaurs lived on the earth for about _____

8 Some statistics show that _____ people are bitten by snakes every year

9 The tunnel under the sea from the UK to France is _____ long

10 The Coco de Mer palm tree seeds can measure _____ in diameter

B Match a)–h) with 1–10 in Exercise 5A to make complete sentences.

a) and cost £9 billion to construct.

b) and used to have a population of 2,000 people.

c) which is 24 times as hot as an oven.

d) and 40,000 of them die.

e) and can live for up to 1,500 years.

f) but 50 percent of all animal species live there.

g) and weigh up to 20 kg.

h) but take between 150 to 300 days to travel to Mars.

i) and can reach winds up to 300 km per hour.

j) and one of the largest was about 40 m long.

VOCABULARY

IDIOMS

1 A Replace the words in bold in the sentences with the idioms in the box.

spill the beans   get side-tracked   left-wing
miss the deadline   get the sack   brand new
give me the cold shoulder   have a clue
beside the point   turn a blind eye to

1 I'd ask Les to help install the sink but he won't **know anything** because he's not a plumber.

2 The council shouldn't **ignore** the increasing vandalism in the town.

3 She didn't want to tell me but in the end, she had to **give away the secret**.

4 After many years of **socialist** government, the right-wing party won the elections.

5 Did you finish the report or did you **get distracted** by the discussion about the office party?

6 What you are saying is **irrelevant**, so let's get back to the important matters.

7 If you **don't hand your work in on time**, the teacher won't mark it.

8 I accidentally scratched my neighbours' car and now they **don't talk to me** when we pass in the street.

9 The little girl was delighted with her r**ecently bought** shoes.

10 I was worried I would **lose my job** after I lost an important customer.

B Complete the sentences with words from the idioms in Exercise 1A.

1 I wanted to keep my wedding secret but my sister spilt _____ when she posted pictures on Facebook and Twitter.

2 After ten years in the company, he got _____ for stealing stationery.

3 Whether you want to go is beside _____. You have to go!

4 He can't apply for the scholarship because he has missed _____, which was yesterday.

5 I don't understand why he's giving me _____. What have I done to upset him?

6 He's a firm believer in capitalism, so he never votes for the _____ party.

7 I was researching my project online but I got _____ by an article about well-known actors.

8 I don't know how he got the job as a primary teacher. He hasn't _____ about how to deal with children.

9 He's got a(n) _____ bike, which he bought yesterday.

10 I could never turn _____ someone mistreating an animal.

FUNCTION

GUESSING AND ESTIMATING

2 Complete the conversation with the words in the box.

rough   less   approximately   can't   might
reckon   way   estimate

A: OK, let's see what we need for the trek.

B: OK. I reckon the route will take us [1]_____ a week.

A: So, we'll need food for five days if we don't count the first and last days.

B: More or [2]_____, but we can't carry too much. There [3]_____ be villages on the way where we can buy something.

A: OK. I'd [4]_____ we could carry about fifteen kilos each, including the tent.

B: You're probably right. So how far will we have to walk each day?

A: At a(n) [5]_____ guess, I'd say about 20 km, depending on how many hills there are to go up!

B: There's no [6]_____ I can go that far if we're carrying a lot of weight.

A: Come on! 20 km [7]_____ be too far for a young person like you!

LEARN TO

GIVE SHORT RESPONSES TO NEW INFORMATION

3 Replace the words in bold in the conversations with the words/phrases in the box.

wow   I see   kidding   no idea   no way   kind

1 A: Endris Praisler has invited 2,000 people to his birthday party.
   B: **Awesome**! That's a lot!

2 A: The school is going to paint the corridors purple.
   B: You're **joking**! It'll look awful!

3 A: So, you're happy in your new job?
   B: **Sort** of – it's not too bad.

4 A: I'm having trouble with my knee.
   B: **Right**. Have you been doing too much exercise?

5 A: My parents have just bought me a car.
   B: **I can't believe it**! Did you do something special?

6 A: What's the best way to fix this lamp?
   B: **I really don't know**. You'll have to call an electrician.

GRAMMAR MAKING COMPARISONS; SO/SUCH

1 Complete the second sentence so that it means the same as the first. Use the word in bold.

1 I've never heard such a bad joke. **the**

That was _____ joke I've ever heard.

2 Mike was really clever. He could solve maths problems in his head. **intelligent**

Mike was _____ that he could solve maths problems in his head.

3 The journey was easier than I expected. **difficult**

The journey was _____ than I expected.

4 The installation was popular. Hundreds of people queued to see it. **popular**

It was _____ installation that hundreds of people queued to see it.

5 The postcards are cheaper than the posters. **expensive**

The postcards aren't _____ the posters.

6 Sarah plays tennis really well. She always wins. **good**

Sarah is _____ player that she always wins.

7 I was exhausted. I couldn't keep my eyes open. **tired**

I was _____ that I couldn't keep my eyes open.

8 The boy has grown to the same height as his father. **tall**

The boy is _____ his father.

9 The dress was so hideous that I threw it away. **ugly**

It was _____ dress that I threw it away.

10 The weather isn't as warm as it was yesterday. **than**

The weather _____ it was yesterday.

VOCABULARY VISUAL ARTS

2 Complete the sentences with the words in the box.

> paintbrushes   canvas   sculpture   easel   installation
> collage   self-portrait   charcoal   watercolours   sketches

1 We started the art class learning how to paint with _____ using paint mixed with water.

2 They've put a strange modern _____ made of concrete in the town square.

3 He painted a(n) _____ every year to show the changes in his own face with age.

4 She looked at the blank _____ with no inspiration about what to paint.

5 He loves painting the sea and often sets up his _____ on the beach.

6 Before she finalised the design, she made several _____ of the building.

7 I hate using _____ for drawing as I always get my hands completely black.

8 In the exhibition there's a particular _____ that I love which occupies a whole room.

9 After painting, she carefully cleaned her _____ and left them in a jar of water.

10 The artist made a(n) _____ using hundreds of photos to make a single image.

VOCABULARY PLUS MULTI-WORD VERBS 2

3 Complete the sentences. Use one word from box A and one word from box B in each gap.

> **A**
> look   call   make   come   shop
> count   give   let   turn (x2)

> **B**
> after   on (x2)   around   up (x3)   off
> down (x2)

1 The children had to _____ a story about a dragon and a dwarf for the writing competition.

2 You'll have to _____ to find the cheapest phone. Don't just buy one in the local store.

3 He knew he could _____ his oldest friend to listen to his problems.

4 Are you going to _____ the match if half the team is sick?

5 If you want, I can _____ your dog while you're away on holiday.

6 Why did you _____ the invitation to the party? Don't you want to go?

7 She tried and tried but she couldn't _____ eating chocolate.

8 The first thing you have to do is _____ the machine using this key.

9 You'll _____ your friend if you don't go to his birthday party.

10 I'll have to _____ with a solution by tomorrow or my boss will be furious.

VOCABULARY MUSIC

4 Match 1–6 with a)–f) to make sentences.

1 I bought her new album last week,

2 The volume of that recording is too low

3 It's not common that techno music

4 Some people find the lyrics

5 Reggae fans enjoy dancing to the offbeat

6 I hope there is some good dance music

a) or maybe my speakers don't work properly.

b) rhythm of the music.

c) when we go to the rave next week.

d) of rap songs a little offensive.

e) which has ten great new tracks.

f) gets to number one in the pop charts.

GRAMMAR BE/GET USED TO VS USED TO

5 Circle the correct answer, a), b) or c), to complete the sentences.

1 My uncle _____ play tennis when he was younger but now he prefers golf.
   a) was used to   **b)** got used to   **c)** used to
2 My dog _____ being with children, so it's alright to play with him.
   a) is used to   **b)** gets used to   **c)** use to
3 When _____ get home from school when you were a teenager?
   a) do you use to   **b)** did you use to   **c)** are you used to
4 He _____ talking in public so he's very nervous about giving a speech.
   a) doesn't get used to   **b)** isn't used to   **c)** didn't use to
5 I've had to give up eating bread and I _____ living without it.
   a) am getting used   **b)** was used   **c)** used
6 She's an airline pilot, so she _____ dealing with being in different time zones.
   a) gets used to   **b)** is used to   **c)** uses to

VOCABULARY EVERYDAY OBJECTS

6 Put the letters in brackets in the correct order and add another word to complete the sentences.

1 There was a terrible smell coming from the fish that I'd thrown away in the _rubbish bin_ (ibrubhs).
2 I need to buy a(n) _____ (itwangre) to water the plants I bought for the kitchen.
3 Each of the bungalows has a(n) _____ (leciretc) on the ceiling to use on hot summer days.
4 I put the washing out to dry but I need one more _____ (losetch) for the last shirt.
5 Your gift will come in beautiful _____ (pwiniagpr) and we can include a message as well.
6 She tried to use a(n) _____ (irah) to dry the wet socks.
7 I used the last _____ (aet) yesterday, so I can only offer you coffee.
8 At home we often use a(n) _____ (rpaep) instead of a serviette at meal times.
9 When I looked at the _____ (icper) on that shirt, I was shocked by how expensive it was.

FUNCTION RESPONDING TO SUGGESTIONS

7 Correct the underlined mistakes in the conversation.

A: Hi, Idris. I've just heard about the cinema closing. [1]What awful!
B: [2]Have you serious? [3]What can they close the only one in town?
A: It's [4]so a pity. I suppose we'll have to go into the city now to see a movie.
B: Well, at least they show original version films there. Shall we go this weekend?
A: That's a wonderful idea, but do you know that the last bus home leaves at ten?
B: Does it [5]eventually? In that case, I'll get my son to drive us. He's just passed his test.
A: Great! Then we can get something to eat afterwards.
B: That [6]listens wonderful.

VOCABULARY LEXICAL CHUNKS WITH MAKE, DO AND TAKE

8 Complete the sentences with the correct form of _make_, _do_ or _take_ and the words/phrases in the box.

| a deal   a pact   alterations |
| a lot of damage   me seriously |
| anything wrong   control   advantage |
| his utmost |

1 Jason _____ with his sister to never talk about the incident with their parents.
2 People often _____ of his good nature and ask him to do things for free.
3 The teacher quickly _____ of the situation and stopped the boys fighting.
4 When the secret of the politician's past was found out, it _____ to his reputation.
5 The architect had to _____ to the design when he realised the windows were too small.
6 If you want to _____ with our company, you'll have to give us a discount.
7 I didn't _____. I'm innocent!
8 The doctor _____ to save the patient's leg and, eventually, the man was able to walk again.
9 My parents didn't _____ when I said I wanted to be an actor. They thought I was joking.

GRAMMAR RELATIVE CLAUSES

9 Join the sentences using relative clauses. Use the second sentence in each pair for the relative clause.

1 Where is the coffee? It was in the cupboard.
2 The waiter brought the food. He was very rude.
3 The film is about a princess. She doesn't want to be queen.
4 I've lost the key. It opens the gate in the garden.
5 That was the restaurant. We had a delicious meal there.
6 There's my neighbour. Her dog is really friendly.
7 What's the name of the pub? You met Fiona there.
8 The police arrested the man. He had robbed the bank.

GRAMMAR FUTURE FORMS

10 Underline the correct alternatives to complete the sentences.

1 I'm totally convinced that the conservatives *will/are likely to* win the elections.

2 The bus is *due/about* to leave at 6p.m. precisely.

3 She thinks she *is about to/may* have the chance to win in the next championships.

4 Do you think it's *bound/likely* that it will rain tomorrow?

5 I thought you *are due to/might* like to visit the city centre at the weekend.

6 He was *likely/about* to close the door when he remembered his keys.

VOCABULARY CRITICAL THINKING

11 Circle the correct answer, a), b) or c), to complete the sentences.

1 I don't believe in ghosts and the supernatural. I need a(n) _____ explanation for everything.
   a) rational   **b)** accurate   **c)** well-informed

2 The product description was _____ as it didn't mention the possible risks of using it.
   a) plausible   **b)** misleading   **c)** accurate

3 Can we meet at a _____ time? Let's say 10 o'clock then we won't get caught up in the rush hour traffic.
   a) biased   **b)** reasonable   **c)** reliable

4 He's worked in the business for years, so he's _____ about the technical aspects of the problem.
   a) flawed   **b)** open-minded   **c)** well-informed

5 The company is flexible and has a(n) _____ approach to their staff's family commitments.
   a) accurate   **b)** open-minded   **c)** a biased

6 That old watch can't be _____ Are you sure it's seven o'clock exactly?
   a) reliable   **b)** reasonable   **c)** plausible

7 To get a(n) _____ picture of the situation, I'll need the technicians' reports.
   a) misleading **b)** biased   **c)** accurate

8 I think your emergency evacuation plan is _____. You've forgotten to designate supervisors for each department.
   a) flawed   **b)** reliable   **c)** rational

9 She can't be a judge in the competition because her son is taking part, so she might be _____ in his favour.
   a) accurate   **b)** open-minded   **c)** biased

10 Your explanation is not _____. It just doesn't sound true.
   a) reasonable   **b)** plausible   **c)** flawed

VOCABULARY PLUS NUMBERS AND STATISTICS

12 Find and correct the mistakes in the sentences.

1 We have raised even more than our target of two thousand pounds. At the moment we have two thousand and two hundred.

2 The temperature in summer is around thirty-five grades.

3 Inflation is two comma five percent this year.

4 His apartment was fifty squared metres.

5 I found the coat on the internet, twenty-five percentage cheaper than in the shop.

6 This car can reach a speed of two hundred and fifty kilometres for hour.

VOCABULARY IDIOMS

13 Match sentences 1–5 with paragraphs a)–e).

1 She turned a blind eye.
2 She gave me the cold shoulder.
3 She doesn't have a clue.
4 She spilt the beans
5 She got side-tracked.
6 She missed the deadline.

a) I'm not sure what I did wrong but she's been so unfriendly recently. The other day I went up to her desk to ask about her mother and she just ignored me.

b) We'd made a pact not to tell him about the party – it was supposed to be a surprise. I put a lot of work into it and she's spoilt it now by telling him.

c) I told her she only had another week to get the project finished and the committee wouldn't accept it after then. But she didn't get it done and now it's too late.

d) I think my mother knew that I had argued with my brother. But she didn't mention it because she thought we should solve the problem by ourselves.

e) The teacher was going to explain the theory of relativity but in the end she spent the whole class talking about Einstein's childhood.

f) Although she has a doctorate in medical physics, when it comes to medical procedures in a hospital, she is completely lost.

FUNCTION GUESSING AND ESTIMATING

14 Underline the correct alternatives to complete the conversations.

1 **A:** How long will it take to fix the car?
   B: I'm not sure, but I'd *tell/estimate* a couple of days.
   A: You're *kind/kidding*! I need it tomorrow.

2 **A:** Do you think many people will come to the conference?
   B: Well, at a *rough/sure* guess, I'd say about 200.
   A: There's no *idea/way* they'll fit in the room!

3 **A:** When's John's birthday?
   B: I can't remember. It *might/must* be in July sometime. I know it's in the summer.
   A: So it *can't/will* be in November, then.

CHECK

Circle the correct answer, a), b) or c), to complete the sentences.

1 We had _____ awful weather on holiday that we decided to pack up and go home.
   a) so   **b)** such   **c)** such an

2 There were lots of phones on offer but I bought the _____ one.
   a) more cheap   **b)** cheaper   **c)** cheapest

3 The exhibition wasn't as interesting _____ I thought it would be.
   a) as   **b)** that   **c)** than

4 The portrait was on a huge rectangular _____
   a) collage   **b)** canvas   **c)** easel

5 I sketched the face of the woman with a piece of _____.
   a) brush   **b)** sculpture   **c)** charcoal

6 You must tell me how you _____ up with such a good idea.
   a) came   **b)** make   **c)** give

7 She sadly had to throw _____ her favourite chair because it was completely broken.
   a) down   **b)** away   **c)** off

8 He knew he could count _____ his friend to lend him a hand.
   a) around   **b)** on   **c)** in

9 My grandmother could never _____ living in the country after being in the city all her life.
   a) get used to   **b)** be used to   **c)** used to

10 That was the best _____ party I've ever been to. We danced all night.
   a) lyrics   **b)** rave   **c)** track

11 I couldn't listen to the music properly because one _____ was not working.
   a) speaker   **b)** rap   **c)** download

12 I bought a special _____ to use in the carpentry class.
   a) can   **b)** hammer   **c)** tag

13 The village festival _____ great fun. You must enjoy it!
   a) sounds   **b)** feels   **c)** was

14 'I wasn't chosen for the football team after all.' '_____ unfair! You play really well.'
   a) What   **b)** How   **c)** Why

15 'I really don't like the way he treats you.' 'Me _____!'
   a) also   **b)** too   **c)** neither

16 You must _____ your utmost to convince him not to leave.
   a) take   **b)** make   **c)** do

17 I'm sure you'll make a _____ if you work too quickly.
   a) mistake   **b)** notice   **c)** damage

18 The thief took _____ of the crowds to escape with my handbag.
   a) for granted   **b)** advantage   **c)** deed

19 I bought the chocolate, _____ was delicious, from an online shop.
   a) which   **b)** that   **c)** what

20 This is the candidate _____ profile fits what we're looking for.
   a) whose   **b)** who   **c)** which

21 She moved back to the house in London _____ she had lived in her youth.
   a) that   **b)** where   **c)** when

22 You're _____ to hurt yourself if you don't use the right equipment for climbing.
   a) bound   **b)** about   **c)** due

23 Inflation _____ to rise over the coming year.
   a) is likely   **b)** will   **c)** might

24 The train service isn't very _____ these days because they are doing engineering work on the line.
   a) flawed   **b)** reasonable   **c)** reliable

25 The advertising was _____ because it falsely claimed the pills would make people lose weight.
   a) plausible   **b)** misleading   **c)** biased

26 My mum was very _____ and accepted all my friends.
   a) well-informed   **b)** accurate   **c)** open-minded

27 He realised she had been lying, so he gave her the cold _____ and refused to speak to her.
   a) shoulder   **b)** eye   **c)** deadline

28 Do you think he'll get the _____ if he doesn't reach his sales objectives?
   a) beans   **b)** sack   **c)** point

29 I can't see the stars but at a(n) _____ guess, I'd say North is in that direction.
   a) estimate   **b)** main   **c)** rough

30 There's no _____ I'd go on holiday to that violent place.
   a) way   **b)** idea   **c)** kidding

RESULT   /30

UNIT 1 Recording 1

1 They led a nomadic life.
2 Computer programming is a sedentary profession.
3 My working day is very active.
4 I like to stick to a routine.
5 She's got an alternative lifestyle.
6 He was always an early bird.

UNIT 1 Recording 2

1 Martha

Could you imagine me then? A busy company director in a smart suit and tie, briefcase in hand, closing multi-million pound deals. It was the sight of those children that turned my life upside down. What was a luxury tour in Africa turned into an eye-opener and a life-changer for me. They were drinking water from dirty puddles by the road and had terrible skin infections, as well as being extraordinarily thin. I was horrified and when I found out more about the extent of disease caused by lack of clean water, I couldn't stand by and do nothing. Leaving London was hard. I thought I'd miss going to the theatre, parties and even the long hours working in a multi-national company. But I've found a much more meaningful life as an activist for a charity, running campaigns to raise funds and working alongside engineers and doctors to try and make a difference in the world.

2 Daniel

Although I had been warned, I never really took what the doctors said seriously. It wasn't till that moment that I realised I had to change my lifestyle. Years of business lunches, little exercise and stress at work had accumulated and the day my boss accused me of not working hard enough – in front of some important clients as well – I just broke down. I even started crying. I was thirty kilos overweight, burnt out and, actually, a little depressed. I've managed to cut down on most unhealthy things but I still crave cigarettes. Needless to say, I left the job too and am happy now running a small shop in the village. My wife is really pleased too!

3 Jenny

I must admit that it's been tough getting used to the change. Being an athlete, I used to train every day and spend my weekends going to competitions, but now it's very different. Although they said that the disability was permanent, I'm working hard to prove them wrong! I've got a great physio who helps me get out of the chair and I've managed to take a few steps, which they said I never would. I find mindfulness helps – you know, thinking about my body and movements and trying to be aware of the moment. It really helps with the pain as well; if I focus, I feel better. After the crash, I initially tried to do too much and was soon exhausted, so I've had to shorten the time I spend doing exercises, but little by little, I'm getting there. Obviously, I'm not as active as I was, but I'm getting used to more sedentary activities such as reading and I've started a blog which I write every day.

4 Jack

It was quite a shock at first. I didn't know what to do with myself, 'cos after years of commuting and a hectic routine, I couldn't imagine an inactive life. You know, I was a typical salesman on the road. I never had a moment to spare between racing up and down the motorway from one meeting to another, and used to get home and slump in front of the TV for a few minutes before bed. Although I'm nowhere near dying, I've decided to make a bucket list – you know, a list of all the things I want to do before I die, and gradually I'm working through them. So I've been on a trip to India and taken up painting. I'm lucky I've got a good pension so I'm able to live life to the full.

UNIT 1 Recording 3

1 I race around doing the shopping.
2 The work is piling up.
3 He took time out to play tennis.
4 Joe's struggling with the course.
5 He had no control over his son.
6 She took on new responsibilities.

UNIT 1 Recording 4

1 Mine is quite heavy, really, but I'm very attached to it because it belonged to my mother. It's not very practical because it doesn't have wheels like the modern ones do, but it's made of strong leather, so it's lasted a long time.

2 Actually, it's not very attractive, in my opinion. It's too big and it's actually made of some cheap plastic, although it looks like metal, and it's got the company logo on it. But I suppose it has sentimental value because I got it after a lot of effort.

3 I find it very useful. Almost everything I need fits in it and it looks pretty as well. I must admit I only use it occasionally, though, because I'm not that fond of mending things. I'd rather buy something new!

4 After all these years I'm not sure what to do with it. It's been in the corner of the room for ages. I mean, it's been in the family for, like, generations but no one uses it anymore. It's slightly broken, so I suppose we could get it repaired and sell it to someone, but it's a shame, really.

UNIT 2 Recording 1

1 Her son made that model. He's very talented.
2 She's got three daughters?
3 They've already been to Paris.
4 He's fifty? He doesn't look that old.
5 You thought it was good?

UNIT 2 Recording 2

I'd really love to live on a tropical island.

The architect created a fantastic model of the building.

There's an impressive mosque in the old part of the town.

They have converted the old school into a cultural centre.

I can't imagine living in a castle. There'd be too many rooms to clean.

What do you think of the design of this art gallery?

UNIT 2 Recording 3

a) castle
b) school
c) island
d) mosque
e) design
f) architect

UNIT 2 Recording 4

P = Presenter   D = Dan

P: Good morning and welcome! In today's programme we are going to talk about an unusual British competition called Shed Of The Year. Yes, you heard right! This is not a competition for the best singer or funniest comedian, but for the most original, attractive or eco-friendly garden shed. Dan Harvey is here to tell us about it. So, Dan, what is special about sheds?

D: Well, the garden shed is found in almost every garden in the UK and it has many uses apart from storing garden tools. It is said that men in particular often use the shed as a place to escape from a busy life and have some time out or maybe get away from the washing-up after dinner!

P: That's a stereotype!

D: But there are also women who have adapted their sheds to a personal use. The women's sheds tend to be more homely and more elaborately decorated.

P: So what do they use the sheds for?

D: People are using their sheds for different purposes such as offices, scientific research areas or art studios, and some have even started their own business from the bottom of their garden.

P: And what kind of sheds are in the competition?

D: Originally, the sheds put forward for the competition were fairly small and many continue to be a one-room space, but there is a trend to build bigger and more complex constructions. The definition of what a shed is, is very flexible but a basic concept could be that a shed can be used as an individual space created for one person to enjoy alone. However, there are also sheds for couples and even the whole family.

P: Who builds these sheds?

D: Well, some of the competitors are professional architects, engineers or builders, but most are simply garden owners who have worked to make their shed unique. There are several categories in the competition – for example, workshops, eco-sheds, historical sheds or entertainment sheds – and people have made some fantastic constructions. There are *Star Wars* spaceships, a Hobbit house or a tiny police station. Walls are commonly made of wood but stained glass or bottles have been used as well.

P: That's amazing!

D: Yes, the 2015 winner converted an old henhouse and added a small living room and then a small shop. In 2016, the winning entry was made from recycled materials such as milk cartons and it had a grass roof. Another winner made a boat shed, but not to store a boat; rather, he used a boat to make the roof of the shed, which is located miles from the sea on a mountainside in Wales.

P: Do you know how long this event has been in existence?

D: The competition has been running since 2007 and looks to continue in the future. It has been made into a popular TV show and, like many talent shows, the general public are invited to vote for the shed they like best. This is clearly inspiring people to become Sheddies.

P: What are Sheddies?

D: You know, they are people who *have* and *enjoy* sheds. A recent survey has revealed that fifty-three percent of people in Britain now have wi-fi and electricity in their shed, while only twenty-five percent have a wheelbarrow.

P: They really do enjoy their sheds then!

D: Yes, psychologists say that people who work in spaces that have daylight, natural ventilation and beautiful views of the natural environment are more productive and happier, so it's not surprising that so many feel better in the shed in their garden.

UNIT 2 Recording 5

1
A: Well, here is the prototype of the new model I was telling you about. It seems to work very well and the Japanese have already expressed an interest in developing it.
B: Great! I like the sound of that!

2
A: So, we can go to the market first to pick up something for lunch and then spend the morning on the beach. How does that sound?
B: Good idea, but you could go to the market and I'll meet you at the beach. What do you think?
A: Hmm …

3
A: The boys have proposed that the council should build a new skate park.
B: That's a non-starter. Only a few people will use it. Tennis courts would be better.

4
A: Oh no! I'm really late for my interview and the bus takes ages!
B: I could drive you to the station if you like.
A: That might work. What time does the train leave?

5
A: What do you think of the government's proposal to provide tablets for all the students?
B: I have my doubts about that. How will they finance it? Surely, there are more important things to spend the money on!

6
A: Where shall we store the fruit before it goes out to the shops?
B: We could rent a warehouse. There are several on the outskirts of town.
A: That seems like a really good idea. Then it won't take long to get it all to the centre.

Recording 1

P = Presenter   C = Clare

P: So, this week's topic is 'learning difficulties and achievement'. I'm joined today by Clare Ellis, who is a teacher specialising in dyslexia, but who has also written a book about how to use the skills and abilities that you do have to your advantage even if you struggle at school. So, Clare, what inspired you to write this book?

C: Well, dyslexia, for example, is a surprisingly common problem. Dyslexic students find reading and writing difficult, so it takes them much longer to do their work than their classmates. I found that a lot of my pupils continuously told me that they didn't feel confident and thought that they couldn't be good at anything. When you spend the whole time at school, you're measured by what you can do in the classroom. But life isn't just about the classroom; it's about determination and ambition and if you have those qualities, you can achieve just about anything. So I wanted to show my pupils and others with learning difficulties that what they see as a disadvantage can be turned into an advantage.

Recording 2

P = Presenter   C = Clare

P: And I believe you started looking at famous sportsmen and women who'd achieved great things despite having learning difficulties –like Duncan Goodhew and Magic Johnson … remind me of the others.

C: There's a long list: Michael Phelps, the swimmer, has Attention Deficit Hyperactivity Disorder, also called ADHD. This disorder leads to children having problems concentrating, being organised and focussing on what they need to do. It means that they may not do well academically but *not* that they aren't intelligent. Another case is Muhammad Ali, the boxing champion. He was dyslexic but he was a fighter – not just in the sport – and well-known for his ability as a speaker, motivating thousands of young people; and he even wrote poems!

P: What was their secret?

C: Um … well, it's really to do with hard work. Sometimes if you don't have to work extra hard to get by in school, you don't learn how to work so hard in general. In the case of Muhammad Ali, this inspired him to help others try and achieve their best as well. He was very sure of himself and said that he became the greatest because he repeated the idea so many times that he convinced everyone until it became true!

P: And tell me more about Michael Phelps; so, he has ADHD … What effect did that have on him growing up?

C: Yes, well, Michael is an interesting case. His teacher told him he'd never achieve anything because he was so hyperactive at school. It's pretty terrible to think of a teacher saying that to a child, but even in those days – and Michael is hardly old – it was not something that was universally recognised. Many teachers had no idea how to deal with a hyperactive child. His mother was desperately looking around for something that would burn off his excess energy. The swimming pool was his salvation because he said swimming helped him slow down his thoughts. Soon he became a rising star and by the time he was fifteen, he was competing in the Olympics and won his first medals there when he was nineteen.

P: Yes, Michael Phelps is clearly incredibly talented but, realistically, not all of us are capable of becoming Olympic swimmers or boxing champions. So, what can the rest of us learn from these experiences?

C: Well, firstly, the importance of trying lots of new things and persevering until you've really given it a go. Amazingly, Michael Phelps hated the water to start with – he was not a natural water-baby.

P: Really?

C: Yes. Apparently, he was kicking and screaming when he first went into the pool – he didn't like it at all. But he had a persistent mother who kept taking him, and he grew to love it.

P: OK, so it is important to never stop trying. What else?

C: Being confident that the traditional path isn't the only route to success. It's a matter of bravely exploring your talents and your interests. Typically, this can be hard for a child, so it is up to the parents to give them numerous opportunities. There are many more examples in sport who show that learning how to work hard – perhaps because you have to work harder than others to achieve the same thing – can mean you may be more successful than others later in life.

P: Thank you, Clare. That's a great point to end with. Let's leave it there. So, Clare's book, *Finding the Win in ADHD and Dyslexia*, is out on Monday in all good bookstores.

Recording 3

1 I have to leave right now.
2 You should've been more careful.
3 Did you have to pay for parking?
4 We've had to make a few changes.
5 I've got a new car.
6 They don't have to come tomorrow.

Recording 4

1

A: Good morning. I'd like to return this hairdryer I bought last month. It's broken.

B: I'm sorry, we have a two-week return policy and you bought it a month ago.

A: Would it be possible to speak to the manager about this?

2

A: I'm sorry to bother you, but I wonder if you could move your car because it's blocking my entrance.

B: You haven't got a sign marking your entrance, so why should I move?

A: Well, you're right, but if possible, can I ask you to park a little further down the street?

B: OK, OK. I'll move it.

A: Thank you very much. I really appreciate it.

3

A: I just don't agree with your idea to paint the office yellow. It's a horrible colour!

B: Well, we do need to paint it. Perhaps another colour? What if we choose blue?

A: Yes, that sounds good.

4

A: This report is totally unacceptable! How can you say that we are inefficient?

B: Well, I did try to get the facts right.

A: You are the one who is inefficient!

B: Can we go through the points together and I will explain?

5

A: Look, there's something I need to talk to you about. I really don't want to go to your sister's this Sunday. She's so irritating!

B: I know you don't see eye to eye, but I wanted to talk to her about Dad and she'll be offended if you don't go.

A: Yes, but I can't stand the thought of spending all day there.

B: Well, why don't you drive me there, say hello and then go to play golf while we chat? Then you just have to come for a quick cup of tea when you pick me up.

A: Good idea!

UNIT 4   Recording 1

1 They'd choose the red one.
2 What will you do?
3 I'll make a cake.
4 She wouldn't be happy.

UNIT 4   Recording 2

1 Emma

To be honest, I couldn't manage without technology. If I didn't have the equipment, I wouldn't be able to study for a degree independently. Because I have cerebral palsy, it was thought that I would always need someone to sit next to me and write for me. But I always had to organise that person to be there in advance, and sometimes it made me feel self-conscious about what I was saying. Now, with my dictation software, I don't need that anymore; and with my headrest controller, I can even turn on the TV without help. It allows me to have the student experience without feeling different to everyone else.

2 Philip

As a teacher, I know I should be excited about the possibilities that technology has to offer, but actually, I think there are more negative than positive effects on my pupils. It has been suggested that students are more eager to learn on iPads than on paper. Although it is true that they like the idea and enthusiasm is important, I don't think

that they remember the content of the lesson any better and, in fact, I'm sure it reduces their ability to concentrate for long periods of time. What's more, they are stationary all the time, just sitting on a chair, whereas I believe children need to move to learn. We often have lessons outside, where I teach the children maths through active games, which, to me, are much more fun and memorable than anything you'll find on an iPad. Also, it improves their social skills and those certainly won't be improved by sitting in front of a screen.

3 Isla

I live on Barra, an island to the north of the top of Scotland. It's beautiful but it is remote and we only have about a thousand people living on the island. In principle, there's nothing stopping me moving to the mainland to live and work, but I love my community and I provide a valuable service as a nurse. It is vital that I keep up to date with the latest medical knowledge and skills, so I use the internet constantly. I'm also part of a connected group of doctors on the islands. We can consult one another in real time about any problems, using the webcam to show patients' injuries when necessary, and give each other advice. My patients feel more secure when they know I have the support of other experts and they appreciate being part of the conversation about their health problems.

4 Denis

For the past twenty years I have worked for a large recycling company and I must say it concerns me to see how new models of iPhones and other smart devices seem to be being produced faster and faster. The old models are then thrown away, sometimes before they have any technical problems, just because they are not the latest thing. It is thought that there is enough e-waste in the world to fill 1.2 million forty-ton lorries each year. Some is recycled, but this amounts to less than twenty percent of the total, which means that there is a huge mountain of waste leaking dangerous chemicals into the ground and into our water supply. There are two ways of dealing with this problem: the electronics manufacturers need to stop making such disposable products and the public needs to be educated in consuming and disposing of these products responsibly.

UNIT 4   Recording 3

L = Course leader   S = Steve

L: OK, everybody. I'd like you take turns to introduce yourself and give us some information about your work and interests. Steve, would you like to begin?

S: OK. Er, … my name's Steve Young and I'm from Bedford. Umm, I've been working for, let me see … nearly ten years as a computer programmer. What do I like to do in my free time? Well, I don't like sport much. You know, I don't go to the gym or anything like that but I really like making models. I mean, models that really work, so things like model planes that can fly or cars that have remote control. I suppose it sounds a bit childish, but the thing is, it's actually quite technical, so it's challenging.

UNIT 5   Recording 1

H = Helen   N = Nick

H: Hey, Nick, I've just read a great article about places that don't exist.

N: Really? What kind of places? You mean like the lost city of Atlantis under the sea?

H: No, it's about Google Maps Street View and Google Earth and the places that should be there but are not.

N: What do you mean?

H: Well, lots of people have seen the Google car driving around with a camera on the roof and I've got several friends who say that they appear walking along the road or sitting outside a café.

N: Oh yes, I've seen a few funny shots of people wearing masks or doing something weird.

H: Yeah, so, the point is that we think these maps document everywhere in the world.

N: Yeah, I always use the app to see the place where I'm going on holiday. Or if I have to drive to a place that I don't know, I use it to tell me the best route.

H: That's right. I use it for seeing if there's a place to park when I'm visiting a new customer. But anyway, the thing is, when you look at some places, you notice that a large section of the area is blurred – you know, it's pixelated, and this article is about what these mysterious places are.

N: Tell me more.

H: It says that sometimes the reason for the place not appearing on the map is practical. For example, when Google Maps was first launched, there wasn't a clear image of the White House in Washington DC. Later it was replaced with an old image of the area. This was to prevent terrorists or others using the map to plan attacks on government buildings; and the same applies to lots of other important places such as prisons in Australia or military bases in other countries.

N: I can understand that.

H: But there are some places in the world where there is no obvious explanation for them being blocked or unclear on Google Maps. If you look on Google Earth at the Faroe Islands to the North of Scotland, you can see that it looks like someone has pasted images on top of others, so you wonder what is under them.

N: Yes, but that may be just the way the satellite takes the pictures.

H: I suppose so. But what about the completely black areas? Some people say they are secret military installations or scientific testing sites.

N: You know, I read something about that too. I think it's really to do with the way the images are taken; and sometimes Google just doesn't have the information, so they leave the area black.

H: Anyway, the article also says that sometimes important people ask Google to pixelate their homes for privacy reasons. In fact, it says that it's quite easy to do – it's not just a service for the rich and famous.

N: That's interesting. Then possible thieves can't check your house out on Google Maps. So you don't have to pay to have your house taken off Google Maps?

H: No, you just have to ask them. The article tells you how to do it.

N: I might try!

H: Also, there's one very strange place. It's called Sandy Island. It was discovered by Captain Cook in the Coral Sea near Australia. For years it appeared on maps. Then it seemed to disappear! Google Maps covered it with a black box first and then deleted it, although you can still

find its imaginary position marked. A research ship went to find it in November 2012, but there was no island at the coordinates it was given and so, officially, it no longer exists! Where did it go?

N: Who knows? So, we can say that we can't see everything from our computer and there are still some places to really explore in the world!

H: Absolutely!

UNIT 5   Recording 2

1   He gave a few of us maths classes.
2   We got loads of replies.
3   She had a lot of cats.
4   I said a couple of words.

UNIT 5   Recording 3

1

A: Have you seen the news? They're banning cars in the city centre again.

B: Because of the pollution?

A: Yes, but I'm not convinced that's the best solution. I think they should improve the public transport.

B: That's a good point, but that takes time and they have to deal with the problem right now.

2

A: What shall we do about all this vandalism?

B: I suppose they should put security cameras in to protect the trains.

3

A: If you ask me, people who drop litter should be fined.

B: You may be right, but we should start by teaching children about caring for the environment.

4

A: That poor man! I'm going to give him some money.

B: It's so cold, too. Shouldn't someone give him a blanket?

A: Well, it seems to me they should provide more homeless shelters.

5

A: You'll have to leave early for the train. They've increased security at the station.

B: As I see it, that won't stop terrorists. They only check suitcases.

A: That's a fair point, but they sometimes search people as well.

6

A: I feel that there are more important issues than worrying about animals.

B: I'm not sure about that. We have to protect nature to protect ourselves.

UNIT 6   Recording 1

P = Presenter   J = Jenny

P: So this morning we're going to look at good deeds by bad people. I say 'bad' but, as we'll see, it may be that sometimes we're too quick to judge that a person is one thing or another. We've been investigating some extraordinary stories of acts of kindness by individuals who by no means have a spotless past. In fact, some of them have criminal records and have faced many ups and downs in their lives. Jenny, our researcher, is here to talk about some of the people they've been looking into. So, Jenny, who are the ones that really caught your eye?

J: Well, the first is Jeff Rochford. Now, Jeff had been in trouble with the law for years, first being arrested for burglary at the age of eight – and he went on to have eighty convictions. A lost cause, you might think. However, he tried to turn his life around and started working as a window cleaner. While cleaning the windows of June Hoyle's house one morning, he was astonished to see her lying on the floor and immediately called the emergency services. She was having a heart attack and his quick actions may have saved her life. Now Jeff is hoping that he might become a peer mentor for other criminals and help them get on the right track. Many people say that he has become a new and better man for trying to help others.

P: So, perhaps the praise he was given inspired him to do even more good work.

J: Absolutely. And on a similar theme, this time in the USA: in 2015 Jamal Rutledge had been arrested for breaking into a house in Fort Lauderdale, Florida. A police officer, who was in a locked room with Jamal, suddenly became ill and fell down. Jamal jumped up and started shouting and kicking the bars. Other officers arrived and began to help their colleague, but instead of trying to escape in the confusion, Jamal sat quietly out of the way. The officer recovered and Jamal was publicly thanked for his actions.

P: OK. So these were individuals who behaved in an admirable way. But they were on their own and didn't have to show off to other gang members and so on. So is that the answer? Do people need to separate themselves from bad influence?

J: Well, you might think that, but let's look at the Hell's Angels. Now what about them for an intimidating group? They cruise around in gangs on their gigantic bikes and look terrifying. However, what you may not know is that they have a kind and gentle side and have been helping children in need for many years. One year they queued on Black Friday at Walmart and then bought every child's bicycle in the store – nearly two hundred of them – and donated them to a charity in California.

P: Goodness! So, how can people be both good and bad at the same time? How can they reconcile robbery and violence on one hand, and acts of kindness on the other?

J: Well, it seems that it is a case of how you see good and bad. There are plenty of people who have done bad things for good reasons. Take, for example, Jonas Salk, who invented a cure for polio, but experimented on his own children. Luckily, the vaccine worked but he risked harming his children, without their permission. So, does that make him a bad person?

P: I can't imagine even contemplating that with my own children.

J: We often think that people become the product of who or what influences them in their lives. But we are all weak in the face of temptation. Can we blame someone who is starving for stealing food?

P: Maybe not. So, there are plenty of cases where the good are bad and the bad are good.

J: That's right. It's not a question of black and white. Human nature is much more complicated than that.

UNIT 6 Recording 2

1

A: I reckon we should get out of the city next weekend.

B: I totally agree. Let's go to the beach.

2

A: The best way to diet is to stop eating.

B: I don't think so. You'll make yourself ill.

3

A: You need to accept your past and move on, don't you?

B: Absolutely! It's more important to look to the future.

4

A: Nothing's better than lying by a pool in the sun.

B: That's so true – and with a good book.

5

A: I think the government has made a mistake.

B: I'd say the opposite. They're doing a good job.

6

A: You should try salsa classes if you want to meet people.

B: No way! I'm no good at dancing.

UNIT 7 Recording 1

J = Jenny   N = Nick   M = Max   S = Sally

J: So Nick, where's your favourite art gallery?

N: Well, if I had to choose my favourite art gallery in the world, it would definitely be the National Portrait Gallery in London. I went to a Cézanne exhibition there recently that was fantastic. He used really thick strokes with his paintbrush and, apparently, he didn't really work from sketches; instead, he made the lines with his brush on the canvas and then put the colour on with wide brush strokes. Of his thousand-or-so paintings, about one hundred and sixty are portraits – and this exhibition was just his portraits. I love the way he creates emotion on the faces and it is so colourful. The only problem was that the exhibition was incredibly popular. There were so many visitors it was difficult to see the paintings very well. You had to stand far back to appreciate them and people just kept getting in the way.

J: Oh I hate that. We went to MACBA – the Barcelona Museum of Contemporary Art – when we were there on holiday, and the exhibition we went to was so busy you really couldn't see anything very well.

N: Did they have any special exhibitions on?

J: Oh yes. We went there because someone we met recommended this exhibition called *Under the Surface*. I can't pretend to understand modern art, but the theme was reflections on surfaces – not just mirrors, but all sorts of surfaces. There was one installation that was a completely blue room: all the walls had blue paint splashed down the walls. It made such an impact on me – I think because it was a very vivid colour. Also some of the art was like sculpture – not in the traditional sense, but with objects made out of all sorts of recycled things. Some of the exhibits aimed to show that what lies behind beauty can sometimes be a bit shocking … and I found some of them quite upsetting. What do you think, Max?

M: I think sometimes artists just like to shock. In New York, my sister and I went to an exhibition of Chinese artists at the Guggenheim, and the most memorable exhibit there was a cage with live reptiles and insects in it by Huang Yong Ping.

J: What was it supposed to represent?

M: Well, it was supposed to symbolise the world and how we live in it, but also the fight to survive. But I really didn't like it as they were caged and I felt it was cruel. In general, I'm not sure the exhibition was my thing – there were hardly any oil paintings or watercolours. I did like some of the art that included short phrases that made you think. The whole thing was about freedom of expression for Chinese artists, but it wasn't my cup of tea.

S: I'm with you there, Max – give me a fine oil painting any day.

M: So where's your favourite gallery, Sally?

S: The Art Gallery of New South Wales in my home town, Sydney, shows off the best of Australian art. They also have the most amazing special exhibitions. There was one back in 2006, the year I got married, which was all about self-portraits, with some really well-known paintings by people like Velázquez and Van

Gogh. Some of the fifteenth-century stuff can be a bit boring, but there's something about an artist drawing themselves that's really compelling. It's all in the face and their expression. I still have a postcard of Anguissola's painting of herself standing at the easel and looking out. It's like she's staring straight at me.

UNIT 7 Recording 2

C = Charlie   B = Barbara   L = Liz

C: So, let's get the event planned. What did you have in mind, Barbara?

B: Well, I think the installation will have to go in the main hall.

L: Won't it fit in Room 5? It's quite big and we need to keep the space in the hall free so people can move from one room to another.

C: That's a good idea, Liz, but we'll have to move the extra tables and chairs out.

L: OK, we'll do that. Where shall we put them?

C: You mean the tables and chairs?

L: Yes.

C: I don't think it's going to rain, so they could go outside, round the back.

B: That sounds sensible. Now, we've got to put the water colour exhibits somewhere with lots of light. What do you reckon – Room 2 or 3?

L: I'd say Room 2 is best. The sun is on that side in the morning.

B: Excellent. We can use Room 3 for the children's workshop, can't we?

C: I'm not so sure. There are smaller tables in the room next door. What number is that one?

L: Room 4. And it's probably better as well because there's a sink in there for the kids to wash their hands.

B: OK. So that's the workshop sorted. Now, we still have to fit in the oil painting demonstration. People will need chairs for that one.

C: Well, we've still got Room 1 free. We can set up the easel there.

L: That sounds perfect.

B: Right, so there's just the multimedia exhibit to set up in Room … er, 3. That's the only one left, isn't it?

L: You're right. We'll need the sound system in there as well as the projector.

C: Oh! Didn't you know? The projector broke down last week and it's still being repaired.

B: Are you serious? The show is tomorrow!

L: If we can't get one today, we'll have to call off the multimedia event.

C: How awful! I'm sure we can borrow one. I'll call the High School. I'm sure they'll lend us one.

L: That's such a good idea, Charlie! Problem solved then?

B: I hope so. Right, so let's just check the plans …

UNIT 8 Recording 1

M = Mark   J = Judy

M: Hey, Judy, do you remember Mr O'Brien, who was our teacher in Year 6?

J: Absolutely. How could I forget?

M: Well, do you recall how his favourite phrase was 'We learn from our mistakes'?

J: Yes. He was full of little sayings, which was annoying sometimes, but they were quite clever now I look back on them. They certainly stuck in my memory.

M: Do you remember how he used to tell us stories with some sort of moral message? Do you remember the story he told us at the beginning of each term about the grasshopper?

J: That was the one about the ant as well, who spent the whole summer collecting food and storing it, while the grasshopper just played, saying there was plenty of food to eat.

M: Yes, and then when the winter came, the grasshopper had nothing to eat and died, but the ant had food to survive the cold time.

J: Yeah. He used that story to show us that we should study a little every day and not leave everything until the last moment before an exam.

M: Wasn't the one about the hare and the tortoise similar? You know, the hare and the tortoise had a race and the hare was so confident that he stopped to sleep because the tortoise was going along so slowly.

J: And then the tortoise passed him and ended up winning the race!

M: The moral of that story was 'Slow and steady wins the race', wasn't it?

J: That's right. That was to motivate us when we were worried about not being the best in class as well, saying we could achieve great things if we just worked hard and didn't stop. I was always at the bottom of the class in maths, but he gave me a few extra exercises to do each week and I got much better by the end of the year.

M: To be honest, those stories were great. Mr O'Brien would always take advantage of a situation to give you a little life lesson.

J: Yes. That time when we had to work in groups and most of the class were really horrible to that quiet girl with terrible teeth. Do you remember? Her name was Sarah and no one wanted her in the same group as them. Mr O'Brien told us that tale about the fox and the stork.

M: Was that the one where the fox gave the stork some soup in a flat bowl, so the stork couldn't drink it with his long beak?

J: That's right. And then when the fox went to the stork's house, the stork served it in a long thin jug, so the fox couldn't drink it.

M: The message was 'Treat others badly and they will treat you in the same way' or 'If you do something wrong or hurt someone, you can expect the same will happen to you'.

J: We became more tolerant after that, didn't we?

M: Yes, and I certainly realised that treating people with respect means that they will respect you.

J: But the one I liked the most was the story of the sun and the wind. They were competing to try and force a man to take his coat off. The wind blew as hard as it could but the man held on to his coat more and more. When the sun shone and the man was warm, he took his coat off immediately. It was a good lesson about how kindness works better than force.

M: Mr O'Brien really kept the class under control. He always did his utmost to teach us to be good kids.

J: He certainly did; and he definitely knew how to get a message across. Stories were the way to do it. He was a great teacher.

UNIT 8 Recording 2

Five minutes later I learnt that there had been an explosion in the station. If I had gone back as quickly as I had intended, I would have been there at the same moment. I went to the street corner where I had met the woman, but she wasn't there.

UNIT 8 Recording 3

1 Redwood trees can measure over one hundred metres in height.

2 The city of Jericho is over eleven thousand years old.

3 The temperature on the surface of the sun is estimated to be nearly six thousand degrees Celsius.

4 Rainforests cover less seven percent of the world's land surface.

5 To get into space, rockets must travel at eight kilometres per second.

6 A hurricane can be as large as six hundred kilometres wide.

7 Dinosaurs lived on the earth for about one hundred and seventy-five million years.

8 Some statistics show that one million people are bitten by snakes every year.

9 The tunnel under the sea from the UK to France is fifty point four five kilometres long.

10 The Coco de Mer palm tree seeds can measure thirty centimetres in diameter.

ANSWER KEY

UNIT 1

1.1

1

1 alternative   2 nomadic
3 sedentary   4 active   5 long
6 early

2A

2 se<u>d</u>entary   3 a<u>c</u>tive   4 rou<u>t</u>ine
5 al<u>t</u>ernative   6 <u>e</u>arly

3A

1 c   2 d   3 a   4 b

B

1 She was a company director.
2 She's an activist (for a charity).
3 his boss
4 He's cut down on unhealthy things and he left his job.
5 She practises mindfulness and does exercises.
6 reading and writing a blog
7 He was a salesman.
8 a trip to India and painting

C

1 e   2 c   3 g   4 h   5 a   6 d
7 b   8 f

4

2 He was bitten on his leg.
3 A lot of work is being done.
4 The cure has been discovered.
5 The blankets are made by hand.
6 Dogs aren't allowed in the hotel.

5

1 had the windows replaced
2 had the walls painted
3 had new ones made
4 had the years of dirt removed
5 had a new walk-in shower installed
6 had the grass cut

6

1 A letter has **been** sent to the head teacher.
2 ✓
3 The photos had been **taken** from an old album.
4 Has **he been** told about the crime yet?
5 Harvey was **voted** the best employee of the year.
6 ✓
7 The neighbours had a large wall **put** up around the garden.
8 The children are **being** helped by a special tutor this week.

7A

1 from   2 over   3 off   4 into   5 on
6 down   7 after   8 up   9 to   10 up

B

1 put up with   2 keep up with
3 hand over   4 take after   5 keep, from   6 put off   7 look forward to
8 take on

1.2

1

1 out   2 around   3 for   4 up
5 over   6 with   7 by   8 on   9 with

2

1 take time out   2 take on
3 be overwhelmed by   4 race around
5 make time for   6 keep up with
7 pile up   8 have no control over
9 struggle with

3A

2 The work‿is piling‿up.
3 He took time‿out‿to play tennis.
4 Joe's‿struggling with‿the course.
5 He had no control‿over‿his son.
6 She took‿on‿new responsibilities.

4

1 is taking   2 need   3 is coming
4 do you do   5 thinks   6 do they visit

5

1 are you closing, don't want
2 realise, are forever complaining
3 are falling, seems, costs
4 do you do, depends, go, prefer
5 is staying, am going, suppose
6 is growing, am constantly buying, have, needs
7 doesn't understand, doesn't realise
8 need, are you waiting

6A

a

B

1 c   2 b   3 d   4 a

7A

1 c, e   2 a, f   3 b, d

B

1 e   2 c   3 a   4 b   5 f   6 d

1.3

1

1 coffee pot, bottle opener
2 necklace, ring, watch
3 doll, skateboard, ukulele
4 laptop, charger, hard drive
5 bank card, key, wallet

2

1 watch   2 laptop   3 bottle opener
4 ukulele   5 pointless   6 football
7 diary   8 lead   9 valuable   10 cap

3A

1 of/from   2 for   3 a   4 has   5 use
6 to

B

1 C   2 D   3 A   4 B

C

1 a practical, doesn't have
  b strong leather
2 a cheap plastic   b sentimental value
3 a pretty   b occasionally
4 a what   b uses

4

1 think, same   2 like, choice
3 must, Definitely   4 Let's, kidding
5 say, that   6 really, sure

UNIT 2

2.1

1

1 flimsy   2 durable   3 novel
4 portable   5 groundbreaking
6 edible   7 clip-on   8 stunning
9 biodegradable   10 unique

3

1 He started his own company.
2 He thought it wasn't commercially or financially possible.
3 watching TV
4 Because they didn't think it was worth reviewing.
5 imagination

4

1 rejected   2 overtaken   3 willing
4 feasible   5 staring

5

1 Could you tell me where **the bathroom is**?
2 ✓
3 Who **designed** that building?
4 How many people **live** in this house?
5 Do you remember where **he lives**?
6 ✓
7 Why **did he buy** that strange machine?
8 Do you know why **he left** his job?

6

2 What should she tell him?
3 Who did she visit last Sunday?
4 How many families live in the apartment block?
5 How often do they take the dog out?
6 How much did his grandmother leave him?

7

2 how often you shop in this mall
3 why he gets home so late every day
4 if/whether they are going to finish on time
5 who you have invited for dinner
6 if/whether you will be available tomorrow

8A

1 Her son made that model. He's very talented.
2 She's got three daughters?
3 They've already been to Paris.
4 He's fifty? He doesn't look that old.
5 You thought it was good?

9A

1 most   2 created   3 truly
4 enhances   5 not   6 sure

B

1 c   2 b   3 d   4 a

10

a 5   b 3   c 1   d 2   e 4

2.2

1A

1 barn   2 bungalow   3 cathedral
4 factory   5 greenhouse   6 shelter
7 warehouse   8 windmill

B

1 windmill   2 greenhouse
3 barn   4 warehouse   5 bungalow
6 cathedral   7 shelter   8 factory

2A

1 c   2 f   3 d   4 b   5 a   6 e

B

a castle   b school   c island
d mosque   e design   f architect

3

sheds

4A

Shed of the Year

B

1, 3, 4, 8

C

1 b   2 a   3 b   4 a   5 c   6 c   7 a   8 a

5

1 visited   2 been falling   3 taken
4 painted   5 been working   6 known
7 spent   8 been repairing

6

1 have finally found   2 have certainly been   3 have been staying   4 have given   5 have been working
6 have had   7 have been having
8 have helped

7

1 have been painting, have nearly finished, did you buy, have never smelt, got, has just opened
2 Have you seen, have been looking, Have you tried, found, didn't leave / haven't left, didn't put

8A

-al: original, regional, musical
-ful: skillful, helpful, joyful
-ous: poisonous, courageous, mountainous
-ish: greenish, childish, fiftyish
-able: changeable, doable, reasonable

B

1 original   2 joyful   3 childish
4 mountainous   5 doable
6 courageous

9A

1 b   2 e   3 c   4 a   5 d

B

1 co-starring   2 disorganised
3 coexist   4 mistake
5 mid-afternoon   6 misunderstood
7 rescheduling   8 redo

2.3

1

1 c   2 a   3 c   4 a   5 b   6 a   7 a
8 c   9 b   10 b

2A

1 B   2 C   3 F   4 D   5 A   6 E

B

1 sound of that   2 that sound
3 non-starter   4 work   5 doubts
6 really good idea

C

1 pleased   2 is doubtful   3 disagrees
4 a possible   5 dislikes   6 agree

3

1 fantastic   2 Excellent   3 Marvellous
4 Awesome   5 amazing   6 Wonderful
7 Brilliant

REVIEW 1

1

1 sedentary   2 long   3 early
4 active   5 nomadic   6 alternative

2

2 had the sink repaired   3 was sent
4 was said   5 is thrown   6 had the brakes looked   7 had a dress made
8 may be charged

3

1 taken   2 hand   3 putting
4 handed   5 looking   9 keep

4

1 b   2 b   3 c   4 a   5 a   6 b   7 a   8 c

5

1 gives   2 are making   3 is growing
4 have   5 know   6 are constantly breaking   7 seems   8 don't realise
9 require   10 often leave
11 are doing   12 are holding

6

1 use it when   2 a bit heavy   3 not too difficult   4 sentimental   5 a bit old-fashioned   6 use it for   7 need it to
A b   B a   C a

7

1 e   2 c   3 a   4 d   5 b

8

1 flimsy   2 groundbreaking   3 clip-on
4 biodegradable   5 edible   6 portable

9

1 where the bathroom is
2 why you took the photo / what you took the photo for
3 when you bought it
4 how old you are
5 how much the ticket costs
6 how often he calls you

10

1 cave   2 windmill   3 warehouse
4 cathedral/church/mosque/temple
5 barn   6 greenhouse

11

1 have moved   2 have been living
3 have already begun   4 have been painting   5 have nearly finished
6 have chosen   7 has been taking
8 hasn't done   9 have been cooking
10 have started   11 have met
12 have been doing

ANSWER KEY

12

1 hopeful 2 reset 3 universal
4 mid-match 5 misinform
6 redo 7 mishear 8 poisonous
9 uninterested 10 co-workers

13

1 budget 2 equipment 3 promotion
4 venue 5 schedule 6 grants
7 financing 8 fundraising
9 sponsors 10 publicity

14

1 has ~~a~~ potential
should ~~to~~ re-do
too ~~much~~ optimistic
that ~~may~~ sound
2 try ~~on~~ the local council
might ~~be~~ work
no ~~any~~ way we can
it's ~~being~~ out of the question
3 that's ~~might~~ a possibility
probably ~~with~~ right
a ~~one~~ non-starter
Let's ~~to~~ look

CHECK 1

1 a 2 b 3 c 4 b 5 b 6 b 7 a
8 c 9 c 10 b 11 a 12 c 13 a
14 a 15 b 16 b 17 c 18 b
19 c 20 a 21 a 22 b 23 b
24 b 25 a 26 c 27 b 28 b
29 c 30 a

UNIT 3

3.1

1A

1 dyslexia
2 They didn't feel confident and they
thought they couldn't be good at
anything.
3 determination and ambition

B

1 F 2 F 3 T 4 T 5 T 6 F

C

1 b 2 c 3 b 4 c 5 b 6 b

2

1 was 2 didn't have 3 set off
4 was walking 5 didn't approve
6 had told 7 was taking 8 was
waiting
9 approached 10 explained 11 was
taking 12 had taken 13 thought
14 got 15 came 16 was standing

3

1 realised, had copied in 2 joined, had
won 3 were living, started 4 had
warned, moved 5 had studied, failed
6 was looking, found 7 grew up, knew
8 woke up, was ringing 9 hurt, was
skiing 10 had arranged, got

4

1 desperately 2 bravely 3 typically
4 undoubtedly 5 cheerfully
6 amazingly 7 literally
8 Realistically

5

1 However 2 Although 3 whereas
4 Furthermore 5 Consequently
6 Despite

6A

1 C 2 A 3 D 4 B

B

1 By the time 2 Although
3 Because of this 4 In addition to this
5 but 6 since 7 Despite

3.2

1

1 must 2 shouldn't 3 should
4 don't have to 5 don't have to
6 mustn't 7 mustn't 8 should
9 must 10 shouldn't

2

1 b 2 f 3 e 4 d 5 c 6 g 7 a

3A

1 I (have) to leave right now.
2 You should have been more careful.
3 Did you (have) to pay for parking?
4 We have had to make a few changes.
5 I have got a new car.
6 They don't (have) to come tomorrow.

4

1 b 2 b 3 b

5

1 studying 2 think more clearly
3 helpful 4 personal 5 respect

6

1 anxiety 2 immersed 3 reduce
4 disease 5 dread 6 (high) self-
esteem

7

1 b 2 h 3 f 4 a 5 c 6 d
7 g 8 e

8

1 moment 2 skin 3 leap 4 take
5 into 6 ends

9A

1 a 2 g 3 h 4 d 5 e 6 f 7 l
8 i 9 b 10 c 11 j 12 k

B

1 one in a million 2 fair-weather
friend 3 see eye to eye 4 on like a
house on fire 5 a second chance
6 stormy relationship 7 clear the air
8 other half

3.3

1A

1 e 2 d 3 g 4 c 5 b 6 f 7 a

B

1 disconnected
2 substandard
3 outdated
4 overpriced
5 misleading
6 underestimated
7 unacceptable

2

1 d 2 b 3 f 4 c 5 e 6 a

3A

1 c 2 e 3 a 4 b 5 d

B

1 I'd like to, Would it be possible to
2 I wonder if you could, can I ask you
3 Perhaps, What if we
4 did try, Can we
5 I need to talk to you, Why don't

4

1 Would you be able
2 Perhaps you could
3 The thing is
4 I thought maybe
5 I wonder if
6 There's something

UNIT 4

4.1

1

1 d 2 c 3 e 4 b 5 f 6 a

2

1 database 2 monitored 3 data
4 measured 5 findings

3

a

4

1 F 2 T 3 T 4 T 5 F 6 F

5

1 awareness 2 platform
3 conservation 4 extensive 5 extent

6

1 If you **didn't** rush your work, you wouldn't make so many mistakes.
2 As soon as I see him, I**'ll give** him the good news.
3 Would you be interested if I **offered** you the job?
4 I **won't** tell him unless you ask me to do so.
5 If you promise to look after it, I**'ll lend** you my dress.
6 I **would love** to go on a cruise if I had someone to go with.

7

1 knew   2 will tell   3 would help
4 don't go   5 will miss   6 gives
7 was/were   8 often go

8A

1 a   2 b   3 b   4 a

9

1 Eyes for All
2 legally blind children and adults
3 to buy (five pairs of) e-glasses (for the local Low Vision Centre)
4 to set up a publicity campaign

10

1 b   2 f   3 h   4 a   5 c   6 d
7 e   8 g

4.2

1A

1 agree   2 suggest   3 claim
4 report   5 show   6 prove
7 confirm   8 believe

B

1 confirm   2 show   3 prove
4 suggest   5 agree   6 claim
7 report   8 believe

2A

1 c   2 a   3 d   4 b

B

1 Philip   2 Philip   3 Emma   4 Denis
5 Isla   6 Emma   7 Isla   8 Denis

3

1 a   2 d   3 b   4 e   5 c

4

3 were reported to fly / have flown
4 was believed
5 were shown to be
6 has been / was claimed
7 is / are said to have
8 is / has been / was confirmed

5

1 The amount of pesticides in our food is **estimated** to be increasing.
2 It **is** believed that the discovery will change our lives.
3 The puma was reported **to** be living in the park.
4 The explosion was **thought** to be caused by a gas leak.
5 **It** is said that we are more stressed these days.
6 It **was confirmed** that the paintings were authentic.
7 Young people are thought **to be** less respectful than in the past.
8 It has been agreed **(that)** the grant will go to our project.

6

1 are believed to date
2 is estimated
3 are already reported
4 are said to include
5 is now suggested
6 was previously thought
7 is claimed to be
8 has been agreed to include

7A

1 principal   2 sensitive   3 except
4 rightly   5 economical   6 stationery
7 opportunity   8 experience   9 advise
10 complement

B

1 advise   2 opportunity   3 sensible
4 stationery   5 possibility   6 except
7 compliment   8 experience

4.3

1

1 footprint   2 screenshot   3 media
4 engines   5 cyberbullying   6 google
7 button   8 account   9 delete
10 updates

2A

1 b   2 a   3 d   4 c

B

1 particularly, Just, Maybe, something like that
2 I guess, some, kind of, I'm not sure
3 really, I suppose, possibly, a bit, could
4 Presumably, Maybe, or something

3

1 b   2 d   3 f   4 c   5 e   6 a

4A

seven

B

1 let me see   2 Well , You know
3 I mean   4 the thing is

REVIEW 2

1

1 He **saw** the accident when he was walking home from work.
2 She had nearly finished eating her salad when she **saw** the insect on her plate.
3 She took a photo of him when he **wasn't looking**.
4 I **didn't know** that you were in the bathroom.
5 Before he **could** react, the man had taken his phone.
6 I **fell** while I was getting out of the shower.
7 I opened the curtains and saw the sun **was shining**.
8 By the time he got to the party, everyone **had gone** home.

2

1 realistically   2 fought against
3 desperately   4 literally
5 amazingly   6 cheerfully

3

1 must say   2 didn't have to look
3 had to give   4 have to answer
5 should have prepared   6 should think   7 don't have to worry
8 have to find   9 mustn't stop
10 should apply

4

1 deal with   2 make ends meet
3 take a leap into the unknown
4 dread   5 is into   6 take any notice of   7 is comfortable in his own skin
8 transitional moment   9 set up
10 hang out

5

1 half   2 stormy   3 house   4 thumb
5 million   6 sight   7 air   8 second
9 shoulder

6

1 misleading   2 unacceptable
3 disconnected   4 undercooked
5 overpriced   6 substandard
7 overdue   8 outdated

7

1 Can   2 is   3 Perhaps   4 need to
5 is   6 making   7 What if

ANSWER KEY

8

1 findings 2 habitat 3 organisms
4 analyse 5 samples 6 measure
7 data 8 database 9 monitor
10 examine

9

1 would feel, lost
2 is, don't have
3 feels, won't come
4 lose, is
5 don't have, don't work
6 had, wouldn't work
7 get, will find
8 won't be, have
9 didn't work, wouldn't get
10 find, will have

10

1 c 2 b 3 e 4 f 5 d 6 a

11

1 is claimed, is claimed to be
2 has been shown, has been shown to cause
3 was agreed, were agreed to be
4 is thought, are thought to have taken

12

1 ✓
2 sensible sensitive
3 ✓
4 economic economical
5 ✓
6 possibility opportunity/chance
7 experimented experienced
8 ✓
9 except accept
10 ✓

13

1 click 2 footprint 3 post
4 screenshot 5 cyberbullying
6 delete 7 search 8 social
9 profile 10 google

14

1 particularly 2 I suppose 3 kind of
4 maybe 5 just 6 or something
7 really 8 might

CHECK 2

1 b 2 a 3 c 4 a 5 a 6 b 7 a
8 c 9 a 10 b 11 a 12 c 13 a
14 b 15 b 16 b 17 a 18 b 19 a
20 c 21 c 22 b 23 a 24 c 25 a
26 b 27 c 28 a 29 c 30 b

UNIT 5

5.1

1

1 rainforest 2 canopy 3 creatures
4 snakes 5 vegetation 6 parasites
7 diseases 8 floods

2A

1 and 3

B

1 T 2 T 3 F 4 F 5 F 6 T 7 T

3

1 c 2 d 3 g 4 b 5 a 6 e 7 f

4

1 little 2 A large number 3 many
4 number 5 few 6 little 7 bit
8 much 9 several 10 couple

5

1 little 2 a little 3 few 4 much
5 bit 6 a few 7 couple 8 loads of

6

1 He gave a few of us maths classes.
2 We got loads of replies.
3 She had a lot of cats.
4 I said a couple of words.

7

1 world-famous 2 old-fashioned
3 compelling 4 slow-moving
5 powerful 6 unconvincing
7 difficult 8 moving

8

miniature furniture and dolls / tiny pieces for the dollhouse

9

1 d 2 a 3 c 4 e 5 b

5.2

1

1 e 2 f 3 c 4 a 5 g 6 b
7 d 8 h

2

1 A 2 D 3 B 4 C

3

1 C 2 C, B 3 A 4 A, D 5 B 6 A
7 D 8 A, B 9 B, C 10 C

4

1 varied 2 made available for the public 3 soft 4 walking 5 early
6 moving 7 not attend

5

1 meeting 2 chatting 3 to finance
4 to take 5 not to ask 6 to find
7 having 8 having

6

1 eating 2 to speak 3 to clear
4 going 5 to climb 6 to inform
7 waiting 8 spending

7

1 **Playing** tennis is something I only do in the summer.
2 ✓
3 The school decided **to give** us a day's holiday.
4 They went out **to celebrate** his birthday.
5 He isn't keen on **having** friends to stay at his house.
6 ✓
7 She's sometimes expected **to work** on Saturdays.
8 The best thing about **doing** sport is the way you feel afterwards.

8A

1 hacked off 2 chatty 3 loaded
4 veg out 5 slob 6 go-getter
7 hassle 8 try-hard 9 chill 10 fit

B

1 hassle 2 chill 3 slob 4 try-hard
5 veg out 6 chatty 7 hacked off
8 loaded 9 fit 10 go-getter

5.3

1

1 unemployment 2 healthcare
3 poverty 4 sanitation 5 evasion
6 housing 7 network 8 media

2

1 a 2 e 3 c 4 d 5 f 6 b

3A

1 F 2 D 3 E 4 B 5 A 6 C

B

1 convinced, point 2 shall, suppose
3 ask, right 4 someone, seems
5 see, That's 6 feel, sure

UNIT 6

6.1

1A

1 c 2 d 3 a 4 b

B

1 b 2 a 3 c 4 a 5 c

2A

1 b 2 d 3 c 4 e 5 b

B

1 inspired 2 behaved 3 separate
4 reconcile 5 cases

3

1 g **2** a **3** b **4** e **5** h **6** d **7** f **8** c

4

1 might **2** 'll **3** must **4** can't
5 could **6** shan't **7** should **8** won't
9 may **10** Could

5

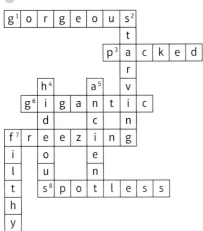

6

1 filthy **2** gigantic **3** hideous
4 starving **5** terrifying **6** spotless
7 astonished **8** gorgeous **9** ancient
10 packed

7A

1 f **2** g **3** b **4** i **5** c **6** h **7** a
8 d **9** j **10** e

B

1 again and again **2** hustle and
bustle **3** fair and square **4** loud and
clear **5** wine and dine **6** round and
round **7** ups and downs **8** give and
take **9** bright and early **10** sick and
tired

6.2

2

1 pursue **2** rush **3** confided in you
4 it's up to her **5** deliberately
6 cheer him up

3

1 salary **2** currency **3** savings
4 reward **5** donation **6** income
7 afford **8** debt

4

1 afford **2** poverty **3** salaries
4 income **5** reward **6** debts
7 savings **8** fund **9** donations
10 wealth

5

1 d, f **2** g, i **3** b, j **4** a, c **5** e, h

6

2 hadn't told, wouldn't have been
3 had felt, would have helped
4 wouldn't have fallen, hadn't been
5 had started, wouldn't have
escaped
6 would never have discovered /
never would have discovered,
hadn't visited
7 hadn't stopped, wouldn't have
heard
8 hadn't had, would have lost
9 wouldn't have been, hadn't saved
10 wouldn't have died, had watered

7

1 B is formal and A is informal.
2 B
3 A

8A

~~Dear Mr Sutton~~ **Hi Peter**,
~~I am writing~~ **Just writing** to thank you
~~very~~ **ever so** much for ~~providing~~ **giving**
a reference for my job application.
~~I greatly appreciate your help~~ **Your
help is much appreciated**. ~~You will be
pleased to hear that~~ **Great news!** I was
offered the ~~position~~ **job**.
~~Please do not hesitate to contact me~~
Get in touch if I can help you in return.
~~Yours sincerely~~ **All the best**,
~~Michael Gravy~~ **Mike**

B

Dear Megan,
I am writing to say thank you very
much indeed for everything last
month. I had such a great time staying
with you and meeting your family. I'm
looking forward to seeing you next
month. We can party in a club and go
out in the evening with my friends.
Send my regards to Steve.
Warm regards,
Benji

6.3

1A

1 is on top of the world
2 looks on the bright side of
3 takes great pleasure in
4 has a good time
5 lives in the moment
6 is contented with

B

2 is on top of the world
3 looks on the bright side of
4 is contented with
5 lives in the moment
6 has a good time

2

1 isn't it **2** don't you **3** did she
4 aren't they **5** hasn't he **6** won't it

3A

1 A **2** D **3** A **4** A **5** D **6** D

B

1 totally **2** so **3** Absolutely **4** so
5 opposite **6** No way!

4A

1 e **2** b **3** d **4** a **5** c

B

1 really cold / freezing, freezing /
really cold
2 unpunctual, never on time
3 salary / income, income / salary
4 a good time, pleasure
5 ecological / natural, Natural /
Ecological

REVIEW 3

1

1 disease **2** snake **3** canopy
4 vegetation **5** flood **6** parasite
7 rainforest **8** creature

2

1 b **2** b **3** a **4** a **5** c **6** b **7** b
8 a **9** c **10** b

3

1 couch potato **2** beach bum
3 bookworm **4** computer nerd
5 film buff

4

1 coming **2** looks forward **3** to tell
4 to find **5** refused **6** walking
7 trying **8** to go **9** decided
10 to go on

5

1 loaded **2** try-hard **3** chatty
4 vegging out **5** slob **6** chilling

6

1 unemployment **2** manipulation
3 healthcare **4** poverty **5** power cut
6 freedom of speech

7

1 about, see **2** give, point **3** think/
feel, may/might/could **4** take, ask

8

1 b, might **2** a, will **3** d, could
4 f, might **5** c, must **6** e, will

9

1 gigantic **2** spotless **3** starving
4 filthy **5** hideous **6** astonished
7 terrifying **8** gorgeous

10

1 wine and dine   **2** again and again
3 loud and clear   **4** bright and early
5 hustle and bustle   **6** sick and tired
7 fair and square   **8** round and round
9 ups and downs   **10** give and take

11

1 salary   **2** income   **3** reward
4 fund   **5** donation   **6** afford
7 poverty   **8** savings   **9** currency
10 wealth

12

2 had worn, would have got
3 wouldn't have, hadn't married
4 had left, wouldn't be
5 wouldn't have lost, hadn't forgotten
6 hadn't been, wouldn't have become
7 would, hadn't missed
8 had applied, would be

13

1 d   **2** a   **3** b   **4** e   **5** c

14

1 isn't, fantastic   **2** reckon, so   **3** isn't,
No way   **4** was, Tell

CHECK 3

1 b   **2** c   **3** c   **4** b   **5** a   **6** b   **7** b
8 c   **9** b   **10** a   **11** c   **12** c   **13** a
14 b   **15** a   **16** a   **17** c   **18** b
19 b   **20** c   **21** c   **22** a   **23** b
24 b   **25** a   **26** b   **27** c   **28** b
29 b   **30** a

UNIT 7

7.1

1

1 least   **2** as   **3** than   **4** so   **5** more
6 bigger   **7** so   **8** more   **9** hard
10 such a

2

1 The film was so boring / It was such
a boring film (that) I fell asleep.
2 He had such a good time in Paris
(that) he wants to go back there
again.
3 The river is so wide / It's such a wide
river (that) we can't cross it.
4 There were such a lot of / so many
problems with the design (that)
they couldn't make it work.
5 She spoke so fast / She was such
a fast speaker (that) I didn't
understand her.
6 The weather was so terrible / It
was such terrible weather (that) we
couldn't go for a walk.

7 My father's got such a calm manner
/ My father's manner is so calm
(that) he never gets angry.

3

1 so complicated   **2** as long as
3 so detailed   **4** such a loud
5 the fastest   **6** more comfortable
7 so slow   **8** such an exhausting
9 as big   **10** the bravest

4A

1 c   **2** a   **3** d   **4** b

B

1 portraits   **2** crowds   **3** installation
4 emotional   **5** survival   **6** didn't
enjoy   **7** self-portraits   **8** sometimes

5

1 e   **2** a   **3** c   **4** b   **5** f   **6** d

6

1 easel   **2** canvas   **3** charcoal
4 sketch   **5** paintbrush
6 watercolour   **7** self-portrait
8 installation   **9** sculpture
10 oil painting

7

1 canvas   **2** self-portraits   **3** charcoal
4 installation   **5** collage
6 multimedia   **7** paintbrush   **8** easels
9 oil painting   **10** sculptures

8

1 b   **2** a   **3** b   **4** a   **5** c   **6** b   **7** b
8 c   **9** a   **10** c

7.2

1A

1 track   **2** techno   **3** rave
4 download   **5** rap   **6** album   **7** lyrics
8 number   **9** fans   **10** dance
11 speakers   **12** rhythm

B

1 download   **2** track   **3** number
4 album   **5** rhythm   **6** lyrics   **7** fans
8 speakers   **9** rave   **10** rap
11 techno   **12** dance

2

1 pop, blues and folk
2 Because the festival grew too large
for Worthy Farm
3 acid house (music)
4 They could watch it on television.
5 100,000
6 under one hour
7 on an app

3

1 unexpectedly   **2** in large numbers
3 without a ticket   **4** currently popular
5 most important   **6** origins

4

1 got used to sleeping
2 used to eat
3 used to drink
4 is used to living / has got used to
living
5 get used to driving
6 used to work
7 get used to taking
8 wasn't / am not used to wearing
9 used to enjoy
10 got used to living

5

1 B   **2** C   **3** E   **4** A   **5** D

B

2 The rhythm of music and language
3 with patterns, intervals and
structure
4 should be studied after school or
(learnt) at weekends
5 and creation

7.3

1

1 tea bag   **2** hair dryer   **3** wrapping
paper   **4** clothes peg   **5** electric fan
6 price tag   **7** watering can   **8** paper
towel   **9** rubbish bin

2A

1 e   **2** c   **3** f   **4** d   **5** a   **6** b

B

1 good idea   **2** sensible   **3** Excellent
4 sure   **5** sounds   **6** serious   **7** awful
8 such

3

1 don't   **2** too   **3** do   **4** too
5 neither   **6** don't

UNIT 8

8.1

1A

1 F   **2** E   **3** D   **4** B   **5** C   **6** A

B

1 stork and fox   **2** tortoise and hare
3 ant and grasshopper   **4** the sun and
the wind

C

1 collecting / storing / collecting and
storing   **2** played   **3** died   **4** stopped
(to sleep)   **5** maths   **6** terrible teeth
7 tolerant   **8** warm

2

1 do **2** make **3** do **4** do **5** take
6 take **7** make **8** make **9** take
10 make

3

1 have taken control of
2 have done tremendous damage
3 take the threat seriously
4 have done their utmost
5 took advantage
6 did nothing wrong
7 make a deal
8 making an enormous amount of money

4

1 which **2** that **3** who **4** that
5 whose **6** where

5

1 who **2** that/who **3** whose
4 where **5** when/that **6** which

6

1 I want to meet the man who/that you were talking to yesterday.
2 My brother, whose wife is from Mexico, got married last year.
3 That's the village where my grandparents used to live.
4 The painting, which had been hidden for years, was sold for a million pounds. / The painting which/that had been hidden for years was sold for a million pounds.
5 That was the moment (that)/when I realised he was leaving.
6 Jeff, who/whom you met yesterday, has bought a new computer.
7 Have you seen the girl whose bag is on the table?
8 They phoned the company which/that offered cheap flights.

7A

c

B

1 d **2** a **3** c **4** b **5** e **6** g **7** f

C

1 at first **2** about five years ago
3 At the time **4** It was then that
5 was (just) about to **6** As

D

1 in Paris
2 He was working for a multi-national.
3 the businessman and a woman
4 she had clear blue eyes.
5 He thought she was a bit crazy but maybe familiar.

8.2

1A

c

B

1 be lost **2** emotional **3** a lot of
4 don't always

C

1 poll **2** fit your agenda
3 newsworthy **4** misleading
5 outcome

2

1 c **2** a **3** a **4** b **5** c **6** a

3

1 biased **2** plausible **3** reliable
4 rational **5** open-minded
6 well-informed **7** flawed
8 accurate **9** reasonable
10 misleading

4

1 reliable **2** misleading **3** accurate
4 flawed **5** plausible **6** biased
7 open-minded **8** well-informed
9 rational **10** reasonable

5A

1 100 metres **2** 11,000 years
3 6,000 degrees Celsius **4** 7 percent
5 8 kilometres **6** 600 kilometres
7 175 million years **8** 1 million
9 50.45 kilometres **10** 30 centimetres

B

1 e **2** b **3** c **4** f **5** h **6** i **7** j
8 d **9** a **10** g

8.3

1A

1 have a clue **2** turn a blind eye to
3 spill the beans **4** left-wing **5** get side-tracked **6** beside the point
7 miss the deadline **8** give me the cold shoulder **9** brand new **10** get the sack

B

1 the beans **2** the sack **3** the point
4 the deadline **5** the cold shoulder
6 left-wing **7** side-tracked **8** a clue
9 brand new **10** a blind eye to

2

1 approximately **2** less **3** might
4 estimate **5** rough **6** way **7** can't

3

1 Wow **2** kidding **3** Kind **4** I see
5 No way **6** No idea

1

1 the worst **2** so intelligent
3 less difficult **4** such a popular
5 as expensive as **6** such a good
7 so tired **8** as tall as **9** such an ugly
10 colder/cooler than

2

1 watercolours **2** sculpture
3 self-portrait **4** canvas **5** easel
6 sketches **7** charcoal **8** installation
9 paintbrushes **10** collage

3

1 make up **2** shop around
3 count on **4** call off **5** look after
6 turn down **7** give up **8** turn on
9 let down **10** come up

4

1 e **2** a **3** f **4** d **5** b **6** c

5

1 c **2** a **3** b **4** b **5** a **6** b

6

1 rubbish bin **2** watering can
3 electric fan **4** clothes peg
5 wrapping paper **6** hair dryer
7 tea bag **8** paper towel **9** price tag

7

1 How **2** Are **3** How **4** such
5 really **6** sounds

8

1 made a pact **2** take advantage
3 took control **4** did a lot of damage
6 make alterations **6** make a deal
7 do anything wrong **8** did his
utmost **9** take me seriously

9

1 Where is the coffee which/that was in the cupboard?
2 The waiter who/that brought the food was very rude. / The waiter, who was very rude, brought the food.
3 The film is about a princess who/that doesn't want to be queen.
4 I've lost the key which/that opens the gate in the garden.
5 That was the restaurant where we had a delicious meal.
6 There's my neighbour whose dog is really friendly.
7 What's the name of the pub where you met Fiona?
8 The police arrested the man who/that had robbed the bank.

ANSWER KEY

10

1 will **2** due **3** may **4** likely
5 might **6** about

11

1 a **2** b **3** b **4** c **5** b **6** a **7** c
8 a **9** c **10** b

12

1 … At the moment we have two thousand ~~and~~ two hundred.
2 The temperature in summer is around thirty-five **degrees**.
3 Inflation is two **point** five percent this year.
4 His apartment was fifty **square** metres.
5 I found the coat on the internet, twenty-five **percent** cheaper than in the shop.
6 This car can reach a speed of 250 kilometres **per/an** hour.

13

1 d **2** a **3** f **4** b **5** e **6** c

14

1 estimate, kidding **2** rough, way
3 might, can't

CHECK 4

1 b **2** c **3** a **4** b **5** c **6** a **7** b
8 b **9** a **10** b **11** a **12** b **13** a
14 b **15** c **16** c **17** a **18** b **19** a
20 a **21** b **22** a **23** a **24** c **25** b
26 c **27** a **28** b **29** c **30** a

Pearson Education Limited
KAO Two
KAO Park
Harlow
Essex CM17 9NA
England
and Associated Companies throughout the world.

www.english.com/portal

First published 2018
ISBN: 978-1-292-21244-9
Set in Aptifer sans LT Pro 10/12 pt
Printed and bound by L.E.G.O. S.p.A. Lavis (TN) – Italy

Acknowledgements
*We are grateful to the following for permission to reproduce
copyright material:*

Illustration acknowledgements
Eric (KJA Artists) 39, 50, 51, 53; Sean (KJA Artists) 10,
13, 54.

Photo acknowledgements
*The publisher would like to thank the following for their kind
permission to reproduce their photographs:*

123RF.com: Adrian Brockwell 11, Boonchuay
Lamsumang 10, Christopher Hall 8, Dmitriy
Shironosov 27, Edwardsamuel 11, Guido Vrola 47,
Nataliia Pyzhova 8, Songsak Paname 47; **Alamy Stock
Photo:** Alex Segre 38, Everyday Images 36, Guy
Bell 48, Michael Simons 25, Phil Wills 36, Stephen
Parker 5, Tyler Olson 34, caia image 47, dbimages
36; **Getty Images:** David McGough 18, Eve Granitz
18, Frederick M. Brown 19, JerryGrugin 37, Martin
Bureau 19, Paul Burns 34, Peter Harholdt 33, Portra
55, Sanjeri 25, Steve Debenport 20; **Pearson
Education Ltd:** Gareth Boden 25; **Shutterstock.com:**
Africa Studio 47, Albina Tiplyashina 34, Alexilena 23,
Artem Efimov 8, Dinendra Haria 36, HDesert 47,
Lella B 47, Matt Gibson 47, Naeblys 32, Palidachan 4,
Tana888 36, TaraPatta 4, U. Gernhoefer 47, Vinicius
Bacarin 18, Winston Link 8, Zoriana Zaitseva 34,
aastock 25, joan_bautista 46, mimagephotography
25, siloto 26, ssuaphotos 36.

All other images © Pearson Education